The Princeton Review

Reading
Smart
Junior

The Princeton Review

Reading Smart Junior

Becoming A Star
Reader

by Bruno Blumenfeld

Random House, Inc., New York 1998
www.randomhouse.com

Princeton Review Publishing, L.L.C.
2315 Broadway
New York, NY   10024
E-mail: web-info@review.com

ISBN 0-679-78376-8

Editor: Amy Zavatto
Production Editor: James Petrozzello
Designer: Illeny Maaza
Production Coordinator: Mike Faivre

Manufactured in the United States of America.

9 8 7 6 5 4 3 2 1

ACKNOWLEDGMENTS

The author thanks Evan Schnittman, for the opportunity to write this book, and Amy Zavatto, for her generosity and incisiveness as an editor.

Others without whose support and enthusiasm the book would not be possible are Amy Bryant, James Petrozzello, and Kristen Azzara.

CONTENTS

Introduction

As we all know, reading an assignment for school is nothing like reading for pleasure. In class, you know you'll be expected to have some opinion of what you read the night, or week, before. You'll have to go over the text with a fine-tooth comb, take notes, list the characters' names, reread parts you didn't quite get the first time. And, half the time, you don't much care for the assigned reading, so the work you have to do to absorb it is doubly excruciating.

Reading for pleasure is much more, well, pleasurable. First of all, the reading is always something you like, or else you wouldn't have ventured past the first or second page. Second, you can understand as much or as little of the book as you please, because no one is going to demand later that you tell them what happened or what it all means. You can skim over the parts that don't grab you, and really get into the parts you enjoy.

No Way Around It

Unfortunately, you won't be permitted to pick and choose the books you read for class, at least not until later. You're going to have to make peace with your assigned reading and squeeze as much meaning out of it as you can.

The first step toward doing that, of course, is *not* putting it off. While none of us is anxious to do assignments that annoy us, it's important that you give yourself plenty of time to do your reading. Not only will this allow you to break your study time into easily endurable stretches, but it will also give you a chance to catch all of the things you might otherwise miss. If you rush through it, you're not being fair to yourself.

We Want to Help Too

Reading Smart Junior is our contribution to your struggle with your less desirable reading assignments. We want you to look at books you don't think you'll enjoy at first as interesting challenges. Here, our four characters—Bridget, Babette, Barnaby, and Beauregard—are dispatched on a new mission. A powerful computer mogul is planning to make printed matter obsolete by converting all the books ever written to computerized text, in the process shortening them all to make them easier to read on screen. To stop him, the four friends have to travel to a parallel universe, the Land of Fiction, and visit the characters in the books they've read. On the way, they learn important lessons about reading and life.

Following each chapter, you'll find a short passage from the book the young friends have just visited, as well as a series of questions. The quizzes are designed to help you look at the reading as a wealth of significant themes, instead of just a jumble of characters and events.

So step right this way, into the Land of Fiction. Hey, you've got nothing to lose, and a lifetime of enjoyment to gain.

Chapter 1
Babette Uncovers a Plot

Ah . . . autumn in New York! As a rule, I am partial to warmer climates, hailing, as I do, from the **sultry** state of South Carolina. But there's something about the crispness of the air here, the noise of the streets, the **blustery** winds blowing down the wide avenues, that makes you want to curl up into a ball and go back to sleep. Of course, being a cat I tend to avoid the larger **thoroughfares** when I am out and about in the city, preferring to travel by alleyway and sewer. One can't be too careful when walking streets **teeming** with humans and automobiles. But, wait—allow me to introduce myself. Those who bear me no grudge, (of whom there seems to be an ever-dwindling number), call me Beauregard. I am a traveling tomcat who spent my formative years as a house cat in some of the most elegant Carolinian homes.

Now I go where I am needed, or where I am least **reviled**, whichever situation is most pressing at the moment. It just so happens that recently there was just such an occasion (the former, that is) bubbling with my young human friends Babette, Bridget, and Barnaby. On the day our story begins, I was wrapping up a relaxing **sojourn** at the New York home of Bridget.

She is an agreeable, if excitable, sort who allows me to stay with her family when I happen to be in town. I was napping and contemplating my relationship with Bridget's parents, a relationship that is touch-and-go at best. (Miss Bridget's parents seem to take issue with my grooming habits and how they affect certain items of furniture. I mean *really*.) As I said, I was enjoying an extended nap when the doorbell began to ring rather insistently. I tried to ignore it, but it was no use. Forced to retreat from the delightful window seat it is my practice to occupy during daylight hours, I took up residence in a local clothes closet and resumed my nap.

It was September 20th, the day before the first official day of fall, and an unseasonably cool breeze was blowing. Babette buttoned up her black cardigan sweater as she strolled toward Riverside Park. She carried a **baguette** she'd bought at the bakery, a bag of fruit, and a newspaper. It was Saturday, and on Monday the young French girl was due to start her second week of school. She was an exchange student at the junior high school in New York that her American friend, Bridget, attended.

When she reached the park she walked down the hill, past a playground full of squealing children, across the **promenade** where people jogged or walked their dogs, and then down another hill to the marina. She found an empty bench across from the dock where the houseboats were **moored** and sat down. Over the summer, while staying in New York to prepare for school, Babette had developed a routine: She would take a newspaper to the marina and spend the afternoon working on her English, listening to the birdsong and the water lapping against the hulls of the boats. Pigeons gathered around to eat the scraps of bread she threw them, and occasionally Babette would look up to see a tugboat plowing across the choppy surface of the Hudson River. It was such a pleasant place to read; it reminded her of certain marinas along the Seine in Paris, her hometown.

Babette took a bite of melon and opened the paper to the back. She preferred to read the shorter "human interest" stories at the back of the paper before moving on to the big national and international news pieces on the front page. She loved the exotic locations, the names of American towns she hoped to visit some-day: Des Moines, Billings, Jupiter, Salt Lake City. She read about hog farming, yacht racing, school board elections, tornadoes. Looking at the quotes the reporters had gotten from people, Babette **reveled** in the different dialects spoken across the country, from California to Montana, from Illinois and Ohio to Georgia and Mississippi and New York. She leafed toward the front and read stories from overseas, from civil wars in North Africa to economic problems in Asia and scientific studies that were being conducted by scientists living at the South Pole. Taking a second bite of bread, Babette turned to the front page.

"*Mon Dieu!*" she gasped, not noticing that she had startled a couple walking by, both of whom looked over at her as they passed. The pigeons were also surprised, and flew to safety a few feet away. "But this is terrible!" She read on, not sure at first if she had grasped the meaning of the article from the headline she had seen. When she was certain that she had not been mistaken, she jumped up from the bench and wrestled with the paper, trying to close it in a hurry without making a mess of its pages. Succeeding finally, she tucked the newspaper under her arm and gathered her things. "I must get to Bridget's apartment at once!" she thought.

✎　✎　✎　✎　✎

Bridget blew a bubble and waited for it to pop before she got up to answer the door. She closed the New York Yankees yearbook she had been leafing through and went into the foyer.

"For Pete's sake, Babette," Bridget exclaimed when she opened the door. "What's got into you?"

"*Gotten!*" Babette said breathlessly as she walked in, smoothing down her hair with her free hand. Her left arm was still clutching the baguette, fruit, and newspaper to her side. She paused to catch her breath. "Do you not mean, 'What has *gotten* into you'?"

"Whatever!" Bridget replied. "What I mean is, why are you ringing the doorbell like a crazy person?"

"My friend," Babette began, "I had to see you right away! Have you seen the newspaper this morning?"

"Why would I do that?" Bridget asked. "I can just watch the news on TV later."

Babette shook her head frantically. "You must see this right now!" She walked into the dining room, put her things down on the table, and spread the newspaper out beside them.

"Babette, the Yankees are coming on in a minute," Bridget said. Bridget was a **rabid** Yankees fan. But Babette was insistently waving her over to the table. Bridget leaned next to her friend and looked at the paper. "What? Where?" Babette pointed to the headline at the top left of the front page. It said:

Wallet Fence III to Purchase Manuscripts

Below that, in smaller type, it said:

Computer Tycoon To Convert World's Texts to Screen-Friendly Lengths

"Wallet Fence, the billionaire?" Bridget asked. "So he's buying some books and converting them. So what?"

"You do not understand," Babette said. "It says he plans to buy the rights to *all* the books. Look here." She pointed to a paragraph down at the bottom of the second column. Bridget read on:

At the news conference in Manhattan, Mr. Fence explained his vision: "It's time to free up space on the shelves of the world," Mr. Fence said. "People can read just as well on a computer screen as on a page, but our research shows that most people don't like to read long books on a screen. So we've engaged a team of editors to abridge all of the world's books, making them easier to read on a computer. People will be able to call up any book they want, and read the important parts at any time, without leaving their houses." When asked what readers who did not own computers were supposed to do from now on, Mr. Fence said, "They'll just have to buy one."

Bridget stood up and looked at her friend's **crestfallen** face.

"Let me get this straight," Bridget said. "When Fence is finished with this, nobody will be able to pick up a book and read the whole thing ever again?" Babette nodded. "Every book ever written is going to be . . . what did he say . . . abridged?" Babette nodded again. "But that's crazy!" Bridget shouted. "You can't just change a book! It's not the same book if you do that! These stories will be ruined! Forever!"

"I have told you," Babette sighed.

Bridget turned and started pacing up and down the dining room carpet, slamming her fist into her hand and muttering, "This can't be. I can't believe it's possible! There must be a way . . ." Babette stepped back a couple of feet. She knew that when Bridget got worked up it was best to stay out of her way.

"We've got to do something!" Bridget said finally. "Come on, buddy. We're gonna drop in on Barnaby. Where's that cat? Beauregard!"

"He is probably asleep, no? Can we not leave him?" Babette asked. She was anxious to get started, and finding Beauregard when he had hidden himself away could take awhile.

"Nope," Bridget said. "We might need him wherever we're going. Beauregard! Beauregard! Where are you hiding?"

Suddenly, the voice of Bridget's mother boomed from the other room. "Bridget! How many times have I told you to keep this cat out of my closets!" At that moment, Beauregard scampered into the dining room, looking unkempt from the shock of being rudely awakened. He stopped abruptly and gathered himself, smoothing down his tail with a few dignified licks. Bridget grabbed a pack of bubblegum from the dining room table and shoved it in her pocket. She walked into the foyer and opened the front door.

"Sorry, Mom! We'll take him outside for awhile."

"You make sure you're back in time for dinner!" Bridget's mother said.

"No problem, Mom!" Bridget shouted, ushering Babette and Beauregard out into the hall.

But Babette had a feeling that dinner might have to wait for a long, long time.

When reading a newspaper article or a nonfiction textbook for a school assignment, the important thing is to finish before class. Right? Well, yes, but it's also important to understand what the writer is trying to say. Most newspaper articles are written pretty simply, unlike some of the textbooks your teachers assign, but the basic facts of the story can still get by you if you don't pay close attention. If you skim over the parts that aren't clear, things that come later in the article that depend on those earlier parts may be less significant to you.

✍ DRILL #1 ✍

Read the article Babette was reading, reprinted here in its entirety. Then try answering the questions that come after it, to test your comprehension.

Wallet Fence III to Purchase Manuscripts

Computer Tycoon to Convert World's Texts to Screen-Friendly Lengths

New York City—September 20—Wallet Fence III, chairman and CEO of Compucon, Inc., called a press conference today to announce a new project, one that will change reading as we know it. The communications **magnate** spoke to reporters in the ballroom at the Compucon Marquis Hotel, and said he is putting the finishing touches on a deal by which he will acquire the rights to every printing of every work, fiction and nonfiction, ever produced, from *The Canterbury Tales* to *The Tommyknockers*. The move by Compucon is a preparation for the eventual conversion of the world's books, plays, and poetry to computerized text.

At the news conference in Manhattan, Mr. Fence explained his vision: "It's time to free up space on the shelves of the world." "People can read just as well on a computer screen as on a page, but our research shows that most people don't like to read whole books from a screen. So we've engaged a team of editors to abridge all of the world's books, making them easier to read on a computer. People will be able to call up any book they want, and read the important parts at any time, without leaving their houses."

When asked what readers who did not own computers were supposed to do from now on, Mr. Fence said, "They'll just have to buy one."

Now try to answer the following questions. It's okay to go back and check the article again if you can't remember something.

1. What is the name of Wallet Fence's company and what are his two titles?

2. Where did he hold the press conference at which he announced his plan?

3. Judging by the context, what does the word "abridge" mean?

4. What does Wallet Fence plan to do and why do you think he plans to do it?

5. Judging by the tone of the article, can you guess what the reporter who wrote the article thinks of Wallet Fence's plan?

The answers can be found on page 170.

Chapter One Glossary

baguette (bă-gĕt′)(n.) a long, thin loaf of bread

blustery (blus′ trē)(adj.) blowing stormily, said of wind; bullying or swaggering, said of people

crestfallen (krĕst fô′ lən) (adj.) dejected, disheartened, or humble

magnate (mag′ nāt′) (n.) a very important or influential person in any field of activity, especially a large business

moor (mo͞or) (v.) to secure a boat, as with an anchor

promenade (prŏm′ə-nād′) (n.) a place for strolling

revel (rĕv′əl) (v.) take much pleasure, delight (in)

revile (rĭ-vīl′) (v.) use abusive or contemptuous language when speaking about, call bad names

sojourn (sō′ jûrn′) (n.) a brief or temporary stay, a visit

Chapter 2
Barnaby and the Ionic Fibrillator

Broadway was as busy as ever when we turned onto it, cars honking, people passing to and fro, some of them darting out of Bridget's way at the last possible instant. My young friend is not inclined to alter her course even for the largest of fellow pedestrians. Either they turn aside or they risk colliding with her. While I am a rather large specimen of *felis catus* (four feet tall when standing on my hind legs), I do find it necessary to avoid the feet of passing humans, who simply do not notice me when I am walking in my normal posture—that is, on four legs. Still, I think I cut a proud figure on Broadway—head held high, paws lifted smartly off the pavement as I went on my way, clearly on a mission of vast importance. As we walked I kept an eye out for a certain delicatessen I had spent time in on my last visit to the city, the home of a lovely little calico cat named Moira. The regional delicacies she introduced me to! Whitefish heads and chopped liver scraps! Creamed herring and beef tongue! Moira knew how to live. I should have liked to see her again but, unfortunately, I was distracted from my search as we passed the Metro Theater, where an elderly woman and her dreadful little lap dog were waiting in line for the Saturday matinee. The pathetic little pooch seemed to want a word with me. Its irritating yipping sounds drowned out even the traffic noise and several heads turned to see what the racket was all about. I had no choice but to face the teensy piece of fluff down, arch my back, straighten my tail, and issue a warning hiss that sent the poor thing leaping into its mistress's mink-covered arms. The lady was a bit put out, but it couldn't be helped. I turned my back on her and her ugly little companion and hurried after Bridget and Babette, who had gotten rather far ahead of me. I managed to catch up to them and the three of us continued on, to the university where Barnaby has his laboratory.

The three friends were a somewhat strange sight on the university campus that afternoon—two young girls and a large, black cat hurrying purposefully past the pillars, statues, and startled college students. When they came to the 200-year-old Department of Sciences building, they climbed the wide, stone staircase and went inside. Running upstairs to the second floor, they walked down the high-ceilinged hallway, the sound of their footsteps (well, the girls' footsteps, anyway) echoing off the marble walls. Although it was a bright autumn day outside, you wouldn't have known it in the gloomy old building. Its shadowy hallways and quiet laboratories seemed to have been completely deserted by students and professors, who were off enjoying the weekend.

The girls and Beauregard stopped at an imposing door whose smoky glass window read "Experimental Laboratory B." Bridget lifted her hand to knock, saying, "Maybe our boy genius here will have some ideas about where to start." Before she could rap on the door, however, a brilliant flash lit up the window from inside, followed almost immediately by a clap of thunder that rattled the entire door in its frame.

The three friends jumped back, breathless with shock. They stood for a moment, listening to a steady patter from inside. It sounded like rain. Bridget looked at Babette, who was mute behind the sunglasses she always wore. "What in the world? . . ." Bridget began. She turned the doorknob carefully.

Inside the lab, it was indeed raining. A bank of dark-gray storm clouds hovered near the ceiling; raindrops pelted the lab tables and the cabinets; water gathered in puddles on the floor. "Barnaby!" Bridget yelled. She lurched over the threshold into the storm and turned her Yankees cap forward on her head, using the brim to shield her face from the fat raindrops. "Barnaby! Where are you?" Babette peered into the room from the doorway, trying to keep her friend in sight through the heavy rain. Beauregard stayed put in the warm, dry hallway.

Suddenly, from somewhere in the room, a **quavering** voice, barely audible over the storm, said, "Bridget! Over here!"

Bridget looked around, but she couldn't see where the voice was coming from.

"Over here! Under the lab table!" Bridget scurried around the table and saw Barnaby, who was cowering underneath it.

"Barnaby! What the heck are you doing!" she howled.

"Hiding!" Barnaby replied. "This is a dangerous electrical storm! Say, you'd better get under here with me! There's sure to be more lightning any minute!"

As if on cue, a bolt of lightning whipped out of the clouds and shattered the human skeleton hanging a few feet behind where Bridget was standing. She dove under the table as the bones clattered to the floor.

"Barnaby!" Babette whined, rubbing a bump on her forehead. "What's going on here?"

"Isn't it wonderful?" Barnaby exclaimed. "It's part of an experiment Dean O'Malley has me working on. I finally figured it out!"

"Have you figured out how to make it stop?" Bridget asked, quivering at another violent clap of thunder.

"Oh, it'll stop by itself in a moment," Barnaby assured her. "Since it's not part of a weather system, it'll just peter out!"

Sure enough, the storm started to die down a moment later. When the rain stopped falling, the two friends cautiously emerged from underneath the table. Babette ventured into the room then, followed by Beauregard. Water was dripping from the lab tables, the overflowing scrub sinks, the specimen cabinets—everything. To avoid all the dripping, Beauregard leapt onto the windowsill and surveyed the scene from there.

"That's some experiment, pal," Bridget said. "Are you trying to electrocute yourself?"

Babette turned to Barnaby. "You mean that *you* have made it rain inside?" Barnaby nodded proudly, causing a penlight to fall out of his wild mass of hair onto the floor and roll under a cabinet. "How have you done this?"

"Easy!" Barnaby cried. "With this!" He ran across the room to where a metal table on wheels was standing. Something was resting on the table, covered by a plastic **tarpaulin**. "Ta da!" Barnaby said, and whipped the tarpaulin aside, spraying Beauregard with droplets of water. The annoyed cat trotted away to the other end of the windowsill, stopped, and cleaned himself again.

On the table sat an ancient-looking machine, a cross between an old teapot and a huge spinning top with an antenna. There was a collection of valves and pistons involved, too, but Bridget and Babette couldn't guess how they all fitted together. Beauregard, who was inspecting the specimen cabinets, didn't seem to care.

"What is it?" Bridget asked.

"It's an ionic fibrillator!" Barnaby said, smiling as though that explained everything.

Bridget waved her hands in a "come on" motion. "Come on, Barnaby," she said. "More information, please."

"Oh! Sorry," Barnaby said. "What that means is it's a machine that can create a buildup of positive or negative particles in the immediate atmosphere, and, on a small scale, create weather fronts!"

"How does it do it?" Bridget asked. "It looks like a piece of junk to me."

"It's simple," Barnaby said, motioning his friends over to the machine. "A gas jet heats up this chamber, which is filled with water. The water boils, and the steam shoots through this valve, which eventually feeds into *this* chamber which holds a nuclear cell . . . ," Barnaby pointed to the spinning top–like contraption.

"Wait a minute!" Bridget said. "Did you say *nuclear*? Isn't it a little dangerous to have radioactive material in here?"

"Nah," Barnaby said. "The container that holds it is absolutely unbreakable, I assure you. Anyway, when the cell heats up, the plutonium begins to break down, causing the antenna to vibrate and alter the balance of negative and positive particles in the immediate atmosphere, which, in this case, is the laboratory." Barnaby held up a long brass wand with a switch on the side. "Here's the remote," he said. "I'm not sure how to control it yet, but with this remote, I think I can eventually use the fibrillator to create small, contained weather fronts *outside the laboratory*."

"You will be able to make it rain anywhere?" Babette said.

"Exactly!" Barnaby set the wand back down beside the ionic fibrillator.

"Well, *simple* is not the word I'd use to describe it," Bridget said, "but nice job anyway, Barnaby."

"*Oui, trés bon,*" said Babette.

"Thanks," Barnaby said, patting the machine. His eyes widened. "Would you like another demonstration? I can make it snow!"

"No!" the two girls said quickly.

Bridget continued. "We came here for a reason, Barnaby. We need your help. Babette, show him the article."

Babette unfolded the newspaper and spread it out on a spot of the lab table that had dried off. Barnaby bent over it and read.

"Um hmm . . . ," he murmured to himself while reading. "Yes . . . Compucon . . . screen-friendly . . . Well!" he exclaimed upon finishing. "Fence has really done it this time!"

Babette asked, "But what can be done?"

Barnaby looked at her. "Done?" he repeated quizzically. "Nothing, probably. I'm sure there will be lawsuits. People will be angry and will try to stop him. But Fence always wins in the end." He took a corner of his lab coat and wiped at a smudge on the side of the fibrillator's chamber.

"But you must know of someone we can talk to who will know a way to stop him!" Bridget said.

"No, I can't say that I do," Barnaby said. "And I have a lot of work to do, so . . ." He stopped and thought a moment. "Wait!" he said. "I did meet someone recently. Another scholar who is sponsored by Dean O'Malley. He's not a child prodigy, like me. He's an old man who's been studying literature for something like sixty years. Professor . . . Professor Thorvaldson is his name. Maybe he'll know something."

"Great!" Bridget said. "Where is he?"

"His office is at the New York Public Library. He works there as a **curator** of some kind. Here, I have his phone number somewhere. You can call him." Barnaby opened the drawer to the lab table and started combing through a pile of papers and junk. "It's here somewhere, I think." He took some bits and pieces out of the drawer while he searched—an old, burnt glass beaker, a calculator, a length of plastic tubing. "Hey, I've been looking for that everywhere," he mumbled, still rummaging.

Bridget looked at Babette, then walked over to the lab table and gently pushed Barnaby away. She shut the drawer and took Barnaby's arm.

"You're coming with us,"

"Bridget, I can't," Barnaby pleaded. "I've got to finish a report on . . ."

"You can change the weather later, hotshot," Bridget told him. "Right now we've got something important to do. Come on, Babette. Beauregard . . . !"

Bridget's voice roused Beauregard from a light slumber. He bounded out of the specimen cabinet he'd been lying in and followed the young people to the door. Pausing momentarily, he changed his direction and padded over to the ionic fibrillator, standing up on his hind legs and peering over the edge of the table. There was a long, brass wand with a switch on the side lying next to the machine—the fibrillator's remote. Beauregard clamped his teeth around it and scampered after his friends, just managing to squeeze out the door before it closed.

✍DRILL #2 ✎

Here is a passage on thunder from one of Barnaby's textbooks. Give it a look and then try to answer the questions that follow it.

Prehistoric people thought that thunder was the sound of the gods roaring in anger when they were displeased with the people on earth. Today, scientists know that thunder is caused by the violent expansion of air that has been heated by lightning.

Air is heated instantly when an electric charge of lightning passes through it. The heat causes the molecules of air to expand, or fly out, in all directions. As the molecules seek more room, they collide violently with layers of cool air, and set up a great air wave that has the sound of thunder.

Thunder has many different sounds. The deep, rumbling roar of thunder is caused by the air wave from the lightning trunk that is farthest away from an observer. The sharp crackle of thunder is set up when the large trunk of lightning forks out into many branches. The loud crash of thunder is caused by a main trunk of lightning that is near an observer. The sound of thunder reaches us after we have seen the lightning. That is because light travels 186,282 miles per second, while sound travels at a rate of only 1,116 feet per second. The number of seconds between seeing the lightning flash and hearing the thunder, divided by five, yields the distance of the lightning from the observer in miles.

This time, try to answer the questions without checking the passage first.

1. How long does it take for air to heat up after a bolt of lightning passes through it?

2. What causes the crackling sound thunder sometimes makes?

3. What travels faster, light or sound?

4. What did prehistoric people think thunder was?

5. How do you tell how far away lightning is?

The answers can be found on page 170.

Chapter Two Glossary

curator (kyoo' rā' tər) (n.) a person in charge of a museum, library, etc.

inclined (ĭn-klĭnd') (adj.) willing, disposed

quaver (kwā' vər) (v.) shake or tremble; to be tremulous (said of the voice)

tarpaulin (tär-pô'lĭn) (n.) a sheet of waterproof material spread over something to keep it from getting wet

Professor Thorvaldson and the Fiction–Reality Continuum

That Barnaby is so forgetful. Without me along, he would forget the Pythagorean Theorem. There's no telling how that fibrillator might come in handy on this journey. It's always best to be prepared.

Now, I'm not terribly familiar with the New York City subway system. While the tracks are good for a quick meal when I'm down on my luck (several species of varmint call the subway tunnels home) I generally find the trains too noisy and crowded with ill-tempered humans—shoving, snapping, rushing off to unworthy pursuits. I had a grandfather who used to say, "Reggie," (I despise the nickname "Reggie" but I endured it because he was my grandfather), "Reggie," he'd say, "the only worthy pursuit in life is that of one's leisure." A brilliant cat, my grandfather, even if he was a bit lazy. Indeed, I have come to look upon his philosophy as my guiding light. But there are things that must come before leisure, unfortunately; namely watching over immature humans who have not yet learned my grandfather's lesson.

In this capacity I followed the three children into the subway and rode it downtown. It was the middle of a Saturday, mind you, and still the train was a madhouse! Not a seat free, and I was forced to sit very primly on the unspeakably dirty floor, ever-mindful of the feet and tempers of the passing tide of, if I may use the term loosely, humanity. Of course, I maintained my **composure**, but I must confess that I couldn't get to the library fast enough.

Finally, we reached our stop.

✎ ✎ ✎ ✎ ✎

Emerging from the subway at Forty-second Street and Fifth Avenue, Bridget, Babette, Barnaby, and Beauregard climbed the elegant, sweeping stone steps of the New York Public Library. Beauregard nodded smartly to the two lion statues that guard the entrance.

"What a beautiful building!" Babette exclaimed.

"Isn't it?" said Bridget. "It took eleven years to build, and was finished in 1911. There are eighty-two branches across the city and together they hold 11.6 million books."

Barnaby was mumbling to himself. Then suddenly he spoke up. "Wow! Averaging out the weight of a book to 2.67 pounds, that's over 15,000 tons of books!"

"That's great, Barnaby," Bridget said, rolling her eyes. Then she opened the massive brass doors and the kids and cat went into the library.

They walked into the hushed main room with its high ceilings and enormous stacks of shelves. There were a number of people reading at the highly polished wooden tables and others waiting on benches for the books they had requested to be brought to them. While Babette looked around, Barnaby and Bridget went up to the information desk and Barnaby quietly told the woman stationed there that they wanted to see Professor Thorvaldson.

"You do?" she said, seeming rather surprised. Then she excused herself: "Forgive me, but no one's been down to visit Professor Thorvaldson in years."

"Is he free?" Bridget asked.

"I would imagine so," the woman said. "Who should I say is calling?"

"Tell him Dean O'Malley sent us," Barnaby said.

The woman called the Professor's extension, told him who was there, and hung up the phone. "You may see him. The stairs are right outside the main room and to your left. Stop by on your way out and let me know how he is. We've all been a little worried about him."

When the four friends reached the bottom of the stairs, they turned a corner and walked down a long, narrow hallway. They could see a small door at the end, and could hear the faintest strains of a song. The music got louder as they approached.

"What's that sad music?" Bridget asked. "It sounds classical."

"It's a requiem," Babette said.

"What's that?"

"It is a song for the dead," Babette replied.

They reached the door and Barnaby lifted his hand to knock.

Hesitating, he looked at his friends. "Are you sure . . ."

"Yes," Bridget said, pushing Barnaby out of the way and firmly knocking on the door for him.

"Come in," a weak voice faintly moaned from the other side. Bridget opened the door and ventured slowly inside, her friends following close behind her.

The room was long with a low ceiling. It was literally filled with books. Bookcases crammed with them stretched the length of the room, and beside each bookcase stood a pile of even more books that had overflowed. Running along the ceiling was a network of thick heating and water pipes. At certain places around the room, the pipes were dripping and buckets were positioned under the leaky spots. Near the door where the kids had come into the room was an ancient rolltop desk covered with papers. Behind it sat a small, old man with white hair. He looked upset. He was resting his head in his hands, covering his face, **emitting** a low moan, like someone with a bad case of the flu.

The kids stood there silently. Then Bridget hit Barnaby on the arm. "Say something," she said quietly. "You're the one who knows him."

"I don't *know* him," Barnaby whispered back. "I've met him once. He probably doesn't remember me."

Bridget hit Barnaby again. "Say something anyway!"

"Uhhh . . . Pro . . . Professor?" Barnaby began.

The old man took his hands from his face and regarded the kids with watery, red-rimmed eyes. "Yes?"

"Uhhh . . ." Barnaby continued, "my name is Barnaby. We met at Dean O'Malley's house at a dinner for grant recipients . . ."

The old man stood up abruptly. "Oh! Yes, dear boy," he said. "Do come in. Have a seat."

The kids breathed a sigh of relief. Professor Thorvaldson's voice was kind.

Bridget hit Barnaby again. "Oh," Barnaby said, "these are my friends: Bridget and Babette."

"Welcome, everybody. Please, do sit down. Rest yourselves. I confess you've caught me at a rather disorganized time. But here, sit down." As he spoke, the professor pushed a couple of footstools and a crate forward for the kids to rest on. Beauregard sniffed around the floorboards and the piles of books, which gave off a very musty odor. Suddenly, he sneezed, sat up, and began cleaning himself.

"Bless you, you magnificent cat. I'm afraid it's been some time since I've had a chance to dust," the professor said. "I do apologize."

Beauregard continued to clean himself, apparently oblivious to the professor's apology.

The professor sniffled and sat back down in his creaky old desk chair. "So," he said. "To what do I owe the pleasure of your visit, dear boy?"

"Well, we, uhhh . . ." Barnaby began. Barnaby was somewhat shy in the presence of grown-ups. "We wanted to talk to you . . . uh, sir . . . about . . ."

"About Wallet Fence, sir," Bridget chimed in. Barnaby sat back, relieved. Professor Thorvaldson, though, sat bolt upright. The chords in his neck stood out and his red-rimmed eyes flashed.

"Wallet Fence! The pirate! It would be a supreme pleasure if I never heard the name again!" At that Thorvaldson grabbed a heavy-looking dart off his desk and spun around in his chair, flinging the dart at a dartboard hanging on the wall behind him— a dartboard covered with a large photograph of Wallet Fence himself. The dart zipped across the room and landed with a *thunk* right in the middle of Fence's forehead.

The three friends gulped in **unison**. Beauregard retreated to a **discreet** distance and peered through a space between two shelves at the gathering of humans around the desk.

"Um, nice dartboard, sir," Bridget finally managed.

Thorvaldson nodded in thanks. "And small consolation, I can tell you, after what that **blackguard** has done. But it does provide me with some satisfaction." The professor turned back to his desk and looked sadly over his papers. "Children, you see gathered here a lifetime of work, an analysis of the stories of the ages. To have it so easily made meaningless by Fence is too much to bear."

"But is it too late?" Bridget asked. "Surely there will be opposition to Fence's plan. Surely he won't be allowed to do this."

Professor Thorvaldson shook his head. "There already has been, my child. Compucon is too powerful for the voices of reason to shout down, and Fence does seem to offer what the majority of the public wants. There's no way around that."

Bridget looked at Barnaby, then back at the professor. She chose her words carefully. "Professor, we came here hoping you would know about some way, perhaps a way nobody else would think of, to show Fence what a mistake he was making. I don't know if you've heard about us, but my friends and I have sort of a . . . reputation for adventure. We could . . ."

Once again, the professor sat up in his chair, suddenly very still, very quiet, staring at Bridget. It made Bridget fall silent, this look. She suddenly became very aware of the requiem playing in the background, through which she could clearly hear the water dripping into the buckets. It was eerie.

"I mean . . ." she stammered, not sure whether to apologize, and, if so, what to apologize for.

"Who told you?" Professor Thorvaldson asked, very quietly. None of the kids knew what he meant or what to say. "Who told you!" he suddenly thundered. "Was it O'Malley? That rhinoceros! I knew he couldn't keep a secret! Arrogant swine!" The professor leapt out of his chair and paced from the dartboard back to his desk, then to the dartboard again, eyes shut tight, right fist pummeling his left palm to punctuate his tortured words.

"What possessed me to tell him? I knew he was a **buffoon**, obsessed with his money and fake generosity! I'm just a tax-dodge to him, but—stupid me!—I began to think of him as a friend. So I introduced him to the Continuum, and now he's gone and told these . . . these . . . *children*!" The professor pounded the dartboard with his fist, and a dart fell out and clattered to the floor. He bent to pick it up, straightened, and slammed it back into the dartboard with a mighty stab.

"Continuum?" Bridget said quizzically. "Nobody told us about any continuum."

"We swear," Babette piped up for the first time.

"We just hoped you'd know some way, any way, to stop Fence from abridging all the books," Barnaby added.

Professor Thorvaldson stopped in his tracks and stared at the dartboard, letting the kids' words sink in. Then he turned around to face them. "You've never heard of the Fiction–Reality Continuum?" he said, still looking and sounding dazed.

"No, sir," Barnaby replied.

"Oh," the professor said, returning slowly to his chair and shuffling through his papers. He picked up a pen and put it down again. "Well. Please forgive me for my outburst, then. I've been under a lot of strain, you see, and . . ."

Bridget couldn't help herself; she interrupted Professor Thorvaldson.

"What's the Fiction–Reality Continuum?" she asked. The professor looked at her, then back at his papers. He looked regretful and tired, very tired. "Is it a way to stop Fence? We have to know, professor."

"Well," the professor said finally, "I suppose the secret's out now. I may as well tell you. The Fiction–Reality Continuum is a spatial realm where the real world is interwoven with the fictional world. Through the passageway to this realm, it is possible for human beings to travel between the two worlds."

The three young friends sat in silence, waiting for the old scholar to continue. When it became clear that he was finished, Bridget spoke up.

"You mean people can go into the books they've read? Any book?"

"Exactly," Professor Thorvaldson replied. "The only problem is, no one can say what book they'll end up in when they reach the other side. One can fully intend to visit Sherwood Forest in *The Merry Adventures of Robin Hood* and end up in the middle of a cannon **barrage** in *War and Peace*. Or in the middle of the ocean, tied by a harpoon line to Moby Dick, the whale. It can be very dangerous. Believe me, I know."

"So you have taken the journey yourself," Babette said.

"Certainly, my dear. Many times." The professor sighed. "Alas, I'm getting too old to do it any longer. I had hoped to enter the Continuum on a search for a method of beating back the evil Mr. Fence. But I simply can't. So I'm left as the guardian of the passageway. I can't tell you what a burden that is. I can't even let repairmen in here to do repairs. They'd certainly discover it while tinkering around, so you must excuse the mess. The leaky pipes will have to stay leaky."

Bridget stood up. "Wait a minute. You mean the passageway is *here*?"

Professor Thorvaldson smiled for the first time. "Of course. I first discovered it while I was doing graduate work almost sixty years ago. I was lucky enough to be given the run of the entire library, and had come down here to the storeroom to look for a book that wasn't on the shelves. Poking around in back, I discovered a whole section of the wall was crumbled away. I ventured inside and found the most incredible thing. But, here, I may as well show you as tell you."

The professor stood and walked around to the far end of the stacks. Over his shoulder, he said, "Come along. It's right back here."

The friends looked at one another in disbelief, got up, and followed the old man behind the stacks and along the narrow corridor that ran between the stacks and the back wall. There was just enough room for them to walk single file, stepping over buckets of water and piles of hardcover books.

Reaching the last bookcase, Professor Thorvaldson stopped and turned. "Before we go any further, I must request that you each promise me one thing: That you will never tell a soul outside this room of what you are about to see. Might I trust you?" The three friends nodded. Beauregard appeared from his hiding place, sidled up beside the professor, and watched intently.

In the back corner of the room stood an old folding Chinese screen with cracked paint covered by layers of dust. The professor took it and pushed it aside.

Behind it was a large, ragged hole in the wall. The edges of the hole rained plaster dust when the hole was exposed. Brushing his hands off, the professor said, "There it is." The friends, who had been waiting tensely for this moment, relaxed, disappointed.

"That?" Bridget exclaimed. "That leads to the Fiction–Reality Continuum? It looks like it leads to the New York City sewer system!"

The professor raised his hand. "Listen," he said.

The friends listened. Faintly, at first, then unmistakably, they each heard what sounded like wind, but wind made up of thousands of whispery, overlapping voices.

"That sound you hear is all the emotions and worlds and problems **conjured** up by all the authors who ever lived. It gets a tiny bit louder every year, as more emotions and worlds and problems are added to the collection all over the earth."

"And one step through that hole in the wall will bring us into one of those worlds?" Barnaby asked.

"Yes."

Barnaby shook his head. "It's unbelievable." He turned to find Bridget staring at him. "Oh, no! Bridget, I have a whole experiment to write up. It's due the day after tomorrow! And how do we know we'll ever come back?"

Bridget was stumped by that one. She looked at Professor Thorvaldson.

"He's right, my dear," the professor said. "There are no guarantees of either your safety or your return. It's entirely a leap of faith."

Bridget thought for a moment, blew a bubble, and let it burst. Then she jammed her hand in her pocket and brought out a fresh piece of bubblegum, which she added to the pieces that she already had in her mouth.

"Well," she said finally. "All I know is Fence has to be stopped, and nobody in the real world has any idea how to stop him. Maybe someone in one of the fictional worlds does. Are you with me?" She looked at Babette, who nodded her head. Bridget then turned to Barnaby. "Are you with us, Barnaby?"

Barnaby looked sick. "How does this always happen?" he asked no one in particular. "Okay. Lead the way."

"All right!" Bridget cheered. Babette patted Barnaby on the back.

"Now," Bridget said, turning back to Professor Thorvaldson, "is there anything we need to know before we go in there?"

"Yes," the professor replied. "Whatever location you come out in a story, that's the place you want to get back to in order to return home. And cover your heads when you go in. It can be rather a bumpy ride."

"Gotcha!" Bridget said. "Are you ready, guys?" Babette and Barnaby nodded. Bridget turned to look around. "Beauregard! We're leaving!"

But Beauregard was already sniffing around the edges of the crumbling wall. Gingerly, he stepped inside the hole.

The three friends followed him into the Continuum.

✍ DRILL #3 ✍

Here are some questions about the chapter. See if you can answer them without going back to check.

1. Where is Professor Thorvaldson's office?

2. What kind of music is he listening to when the kids visit him?

3. What kind of animal does Professor Thorvaldson compare Dean O'Malley to when he gets angry?

4. Why is he so angry at Dean O'Malley?

5. What color is Professor Thorvaldson's hair?

The answers can be found on page 170.

Chapter Three Glossary

barrage (bär′ ĭj) (n.) a curtain of artillery fire laid down to prevent enemy forces from moving, or to cover one's own forces; a heavy, prolonged attack of words, blows, etc.

blackguard (blăg′ ərd) (n.) scoundrel; villain

buffoon (bə-fōōn′) (n.) a person who is always clowning and trying to be funny; clown

composure (kəm-pō′zhər) (n.) calmness of mind or manner; tranquillity; self-possession

conjure (kŏn′ jər) (v.) call to mind; summon (in primitive religious rites) by magic

discreet (dĭ-skrēt′) (adj.) having or showing good judgment

emit (ĭ-mĭt′) (v.) to send out, give forth, discharge

prim (prĭm) (adj.) stiffly formal, precise, moral, proper

unison (yōōn′ nĭ-sən) (adj.) at the same time; together

varmint (vär′ mĭnt) (n.) a person or animal regarded as troublesome or objectionable

Chapter 4
A Trip Down the Mississippi River

They say that cats always land on their feet. If only it were true! Of course, it's hard to figure out where you're going to land when you're falling through pitch darkness and you don't know which way is up. After a few steps through the hole in the wall, I seemed to be on a very steep hill of dirt and gravel and couldn't gain a secure footing. I slid several feet, scrambling to right myself, and then suddenly came to the edge — but the edge of *what* I did not know. Without so much as a chance to try to hold on, I was off the edge and hurtling through this inky blackness, with that unsettling wind howling in my ears. The fall took ages, and I'm afraid I got quite **ruffled** trying to turn this way and that so that I could be assured of being upright. Above the wind, I could hear the yelps and calls of my three young companions. They were apparently experiencing emotions similar to my own, but were giving voice to their concerns in ways that I never would.

Just when I thought I might, out of anxiety, emit an undignified howl, I was flat on my back on a hard, even surface. I got up as fast as I could and scrambled away from the spot where I had fallen, for I had no doubt that, had I not done so, I would be squashed by falling human bodies. I smoothed my fur as best I could and awaited their arrival. I hadn't long to wait!

✎ ✎ ✎ ✎ ✎

"Ow!" Bridget groaned. "Barnaby, you're on my leg!"

"Sorry," Barnaby said. He tried to get up, but he was having difficulty, tangled up as he was with Babette. The French girl straightened her sunglasses and freed herself from the pile. She brushed herself off.

"*Zut alors!*" Babette said, **lapsing** briefly into her native tongue. "That was a long fall!"

"I'll say," Barnaby said. "I wonder where we are." He stood up and immediately hit his head. "Ouch! Low ceiling!" The brass fibrillator's remote fell out of Barnaby's hair and clattered to the floor. He picked it up and put it in the pocket of his lab coat, rubbing his head.

Bridget got up too. "That's not a ceiling! It's a mantelpiece! We fell into the fireplace of someone's house." The three kids looked around. They really were in one of the rooms of a house. There were two armchairs, a table, a bed, and a door leading off to other rooms. It all looked very old somehow. The walls were stained and peeling, and the floor was covered with dust.

"Good thing no one built a fire for the occasion," Barnaby commented.

"Perhaps we should find a hiding place," Babette suggested, "in case the occupants are at home."

Bridget put her hands on her hips and looked around. "I don't know. It seems quiet. Let's investigate."

At that moment, the house gave a shudder and the floor shifted under the kids' feet. Beauregard, who was busy settling into one of the armchairs, stopped and looked around uneasily.

"What's going on?" Barnaby said. The floor seemed slightly tilted. The kids had to adjust to keep their balance.

"Is it an earthquake?" Babette asked. She'd never been in an earthquake before.

"I don't think so," Bridget said. She wobbled over to the window and held onto the windowsill. "Um . . . guys? You'd better come look at this." Babette walked carefully over to where Bridget was standing and Barnaby followed suit. They looked out the window.

They were surrounded by water. They all looked down and saw that they were on the second story of a house that was partially submerged in what appeared to be a brown-colored river—and they were moving downstream.

"We're floating down a river, guys," Bridget said. "Look across there and you can see the shore."

Babette and Barnaby looked and, far away, they could see a riverbank lined with trees and heavy brush.

"How is this possible?" Babette asked. "Is it a houseboat?"

Bridget shook her head. "No such luck. Probably it stormed recently, the river rose, and the house was washed off from wherever it was standing."

"Well, shouldn't we get out of it before it falls over and sinks?" Barnaby asked.

"That's not a bad idea," Bridget answered. "How good a swimmer are you? Can you make that shore?"

Barnaby frowned. "Um, well. Probably not," he said.

"And we know how Beauregard loves to get wet," Bridget said.

"Bridget!" Babette said suddenly from across the room. She was looking out the other window. "There is a boy paddling by in a canoe!"

Bridget ran over. "Call him! He can rescue us!"

"Hey!" Babette called. Bridget looked out the window. The boy was paddling away pretty slowly. He didn't seem to have heard Babette's call.

"Hey you!" Bridget **bellowed**, with considerably more power than Babette could muster. "Over here!"

The boy in the canoe turned and looked over his shoulder. Then he turned back and began paddling frantically for a small island in the middle of the river. He was an expert at it, and in a moment he was halfway to the island.

"Come back!" Bridget said. "Please! We won't hurt you! We need your help!"

The boy didn't seem interested in stopping. But then, suddenly, he did. He stopped paddling, laid the oar across his lap and looked back at the house. Motionless, he seemed to reconsider something.

"Come on, kid," Bridget said under her breath. "Turn around already."

Incredibly, the boy put his paddle in the water and started to turn back.

"Hooray!" Bridget yelled. "He's coming back!"

"Thank goodness," Babette said.

The boy paddled up alongside the house. He had squinty eyes and was wearing an old pair of overalls. "What're you folks doin' in there?" he said. "I just clumb in the window to look aroun' and I didn't see nobody." The boy had a bunch of old clothes and blankets piled in the bottom of his boat.

"Uhh . . . we just got here ourselves," Bridget said. "Look, it's kind of a long story. Can you help us get out of here?"

"I reckon so," the boy said, "if you won't tell nobody you seen me."

"Why?" Barnaby asked.

"Quiet, Barnaby," Bridget said. She turned back to the boy in the canoe. "We promise. We won't tell a soul."

"Get on in, then," the boy said. He braced himself against the side of the house. Babette climbed out the window first, followed by Barnaby, Bridget, and, finally, Beauregard.

"Whoa!" the kid exclaimed. "Thas the biggest, blackest cat I ever seen! Jim'd be mighty 'fraid a him, account of his superstitious."

"Who's Jim?" Bridget asked, forgetting that she shouldn't ask too many questions. The boy seemed kind of secretive.

As Bridget expected, the boy was quiet for a moment as he pushed off from the house. "Well, Jim, he's . . ." he said, "he's just a frien'. I guess thas all I'll say."

"Well," Bridget said, "my name's Bridget, and these are my friends Babette and Barnaby."

"Hello," Babette said.

"Hi," said Barnaby. The boy just nodded.

The river was wide and the water was high and calm. The young boy paddled with a gentle current that pushed them toward the bottom-most point of the island, which was thick with deep green trees and bushes. Babette looked back along the shore they were moving away from and saw some lights from houses there.

The canoe was coming up to the island. "You folks duck yer heads," the boy said. "I'm gonna come up under that brush there."

The three kids did as they were told, and the canoe slipped in next to the bank of the island. The boy in overalls jumped out into the shallow water and pulled the canoe halfway onto shore. Everybody climbed out, including Beauregard.

"I got me a campsite up on the ridge a ways," the kid said. "Come on."

They all followed him up the hill, Bridget first, then Babette, with Barnaby and Beauregard bringing up the rear. The island was overgrown and swampy in places, but they soon came to the clearing where the campsite was. Everyone sat down. The kid in overalls had a fire going in no time, and sat down himself.

"So what brings you here?" he said to the three friends. "I don't reckon I seen none a you before. You from down Goshen?"

"Not exactly," Bridget said. "Before we get into that, can you tell us where we are?"

"Well," the boy said, "that sorta depends what side of the river you cling to. Over there on the Illinois side is Hookerville." He pointed the way they had come, then pointed back over his shoulder with his thumb, saying, "And that over there is the Missouri side."

"What river is this?" Babette asked.

"Why, it's the Mississippi, of course," the boy laughed.

Barnaby jumped up. "You're Huck Finn!" he blurted.

Everybody was startled, not least the boy who'd been accused of being Huck Finn. He stood up himself.

"I guess you got me," he said.

"Barnaby! Sit down!" Bridget said. Barnaby did.

"So who sent you?" Huck demanded. "The Widow Douglas? Are you out to find Jim and claim the reward? Come on, speak up!"

Bridget stood up herself. "Look," she said, "we're not here to look for you or get a reward. We're sort of on a mission. Maybe you can help us."

"Well, if you ain't lookin' fer me, then how's your frien' know my name?" Huck wanted to know.

Bridget looked at Barnaby with annoyance. Barnaby shrugged.

"You'll have to forgive him," Bridget said. "But where we come from, you're pretty famous."

Huck stroked his chin and nodded, looking into the fire. "Yeah, I guess I'm well-known around these parts too," he said. "Too well-known for my own good." He looked up. "So where'd you say you was from, anyway?"

Bridget hesitated, then decided to tell some of the truth, but not all of it. "Well, Barnaby and I are from New York, and Babette's from Paris, France."

"No kiddin'?" Huck said. "They know about me in all them places?" The three friends nodded. "I know Mr. Twain wrote about me and Tom Sawyer in a book about Tom, but I didn't know people read it as far away as that. Man alive, what kinda mission could make you come all the way here?"

"It's kind of hard to explain," Bridget said. "But there's a very powerful man back home who wants to shorten all the books, and we want to find a way to stop him."

"He sounds like a right sensible fellow," Huck replied. "He can burn 'em all while he's at it. I never run acrost a book I had any use for."

"But you don't understand," Bridget said. "If this man gets his way, a lot of the things you know will disappear."

Huck laughed. "Like the Widow Douglas and Miss Watson? I hope they'll be first in line. He can have Pap too."

"Like maybe Tom and Jim and Mary Jane and even the King!" Barnaby spoke up.

"What?" Huck said. "Who're Mary Jane and the King? What're you talkin' about?"

"Barnaby," Bridget said, closing her eyes in frustration. "He hasn't met those people yet."

"Oh. Sorry," Barnaby said.

"I haven't met?" Huck said. "Listen, tell me what's goin' on here. I'm startin' to get riled."

Bridget paused. "Okay," she said. "You see, where we come from there's a book about you that's not about Tom Sawyer. I mean, he's in it, but it's really about you. And in it you escape from your father's shack and hide out on this island . . ."

"Which I did," Huck said.

"Right," Bridget said. "But the book also tells about you taking a rafting trip down the river, and meeting a lot of different people."

"How's it end?" Huck asked.

"Well," Bridget said. "What's important is that this man back in . . . where we come from . . . has the power to eliminate parts of your life, so that they won't exist."

"I see," Huck said. He sat thinking. "But if all this ain't happened yet, the stuff you say is gonna happen, can't I change what happens by acting different than I would if I did what the book says?"

"But we don't have time to tell you the whole book," Bridget replied. "We need to find a way to stop the man who wants to change the book and get home before it's too late."

"Well, I don't know," Huck said.

"So, you can't help us?" Babette said.

"I didn't say that. Lemme see," Huck said, thinking. "You could put a rattlesnake in his bed. Or you could kidnap him and tell him to stop and think real hard about what he's doing before you turn him loose. You could even get a ransom out of it maybe. Tom Sawyer and me started a band of outlaws and we was gonna do some kidnappings but we never got around to 'em."

Bridget sighed. "That's out of the question, Huck," she said.

"Well, I don't know then," Huck said. Then he brightened. "Wait! Jim might know a spell or two. He knows a whole mess of spells."

"Jim, huh? Now where would he be hiding at?" said a voice that was gruff and mean. The four kids turned around to see two men with rifles. The rifles were pointed in the kids' direction.

Huck stood up. "I don't know what yer talkin' about, mister," he said.

The larger man answered. "You don't, huh? You'd be Huck Finn, wouldn't you? Ever'body thinks you're dead and Jim done it. Now you want to come along with us and take us to him? There's a reward for us to c'lect."

"I tell you I don't know where he is," Huck insisted. The men cocked the hammers on their rifles.

"We think you do," the man said. "And we think you'll do what we tell you. Unless you want the rumors of your death to come true."

Huck didn't move. Nobody did. The fire crackled.

Suddenly a screech tore through the clearing. Babette had grabbed Beauregard and heaved him at the two men, who were too surprised to do anything. Beauregard's full, furry weight landed in the first man's face, backed up by claws and teeth. The man dropped his weapon and used his hands to pry Beauregard off of his head. Babette leapt forward and, yelling "Hi-*yah!*" kicked the rifle out of the other man's hands. Then she kicked him again, hard, in the center of his chest, laying him out on his back in the dust. Huck grabbed one of the guns. The other had fallen at Barnaby's feet. Barnaby bent down and, with trembling hands, picked up the rifle.

"You boys get," Huck said.

The man Beauregard had **mauled** wasn't convinced. "Why you little pip-squeak," he said to Barnaby. "Gimme that gun!"

Barnaby froze. The man advanced.

Huck yelled, "Don't go no closer, mister!" The man stopped and turned toward Huck.

"Who's gonna stop me?" he said. "You?" He turned to Barnaby and glared, red-eyed, his face covered with scratches. He took another step toward Barnaby and pulled a big knife out of his belt. The knife's sharp, steel blade made a faint ringing sound when it came out of the belt. The kids gulped. Barnaby backed slowly away and closed his eyes.

With a deafening boom, the gun went off in Barnaby's hands and everybody hit the deck. Barnaby fell on his back and dropped the gun. The two men turned and ran into the bushes, yelling. A moment later, the kids heard them jump into the river. They were on the run.

Huck fired *his* gun into the air for good measure. "Yahoo!" he yelled. "That was some fightin'! I never seen the like before!"

"It is karate," Babette said softly.

"I don't care if it's alligator wrestlin'," Huck said. "It's okay with me. And, Barnaby, yer a master with a scatter gun!"

Barnaby was still trembling all over. "Th–thanks," he managed.

"Well, I wish I could help you folks since you helped me," Huck said. "I can get you one of Jim's spells for beatin' away evil spirits. I don't put much store in 'em, but maybe it'll do somethin'. It's time for Jim an' me to start down river. Those hogs'll sound the alarm pretty soon. How're you planning on gettin' home?"

"Just get us back to that floating house please," Bridget said. "We'll take it from there."

"If you say so," Huck said. "Let's get on down to the canoe."

The house had floated about a half mile downriver. When the canoe pulled up alongside it, darkness was falling on the Illinois side. Beauregard jumped up to the windowsill.

"Careful getting up there," Huck warned. "You better not stay in the house too long. She's gonna fall over." He took a scrap of paper from the bib of his overalls. "Here's the spell I wrote down from Jim tellin' it to me." He gave the paper to Bridget.

"Thanks!" Bridget said. "And good luck!" She climbed in the window, with Babette right after her.

Barnaby said, "It was a pleasure meeting you." He climbed up then, too.

"Pleasure's all mine. I reckon you saved my life," Huck said, and pushed off from the side of the house. The three friends watched him through the window for a moment as he paddled away.

Bridget stepped back from the window and scratched her head. "Well, that was terrifying, and we're no closer to our goal than we were before, except for this dumb spell. I hate to go home empty-handed."

"Not me!" Barnaby shouted. "I'll go home any way at all! Where's that fireplace?"

It was dim in the room, but they could see Beauregard sitting on the mantelpiece. He jumped down, stepped into the fireplace, and was gone.

"Beauregard!" Bridget yelled. She ran over to the hearth. "Beauregard, where did you go?" She knelt down and ran her hands over the stone floor of the fireplace. "Hey, there's a grate back here that's been pushed aside. This must be the way back!"

"Let me at it," Barnaby said. He eased himself down into the chute. Supporting himself with his elbows, he let his legs dangle. "See you in New York!" he said. Then he dropped out of sight. The two girls followed him, as eager to get home as Barnaby was.

In his book, *The Adventures of Huckleberry Finn*, Mark Twain wrote in the language spoken by people who lived along certain parts of the Mississippi River in the nineteenth century. Here's a passage from the book in which Huck, who is living in the Widow Douglas's house, is paid a visit by his father:

> I had shut the door to. Then I turned around, and there he was. I used to be scared of him all the time, he tanned me so much. I reckoned I was scared of him now, too; but in a minute I see I was mistaken—that is, after the first jolt, as you may say, when my breath sort of hitched, he being so unexpected; but right away after I see I warn't scared of him worth bothering about.
>
> He was most fifty, and he looked it. His hair was long and tangled and greasy, and hung down, and

you could see his eyes shining through like he was behind vines. It was all black, no gray; so was his long, mixed-up whiskers. There warn't no color in his face, where his face showed; it was white; not like another man's white, but a white to make a body sick, a white to make a body's flesh crawl— a tree-toad white, a fish-belly white. As for his clothes—just rags, that was all. He had one ankle resting on t'other knee; the boot on that foot was busted, and two of his toes stuck through, and he worked them now and then. His hat was laying on the floor—an old black slouch with the top caved in, like a lid.

I stood a-looking at him. He set there a-looking at me, with his chair tilted back a little. I set the candle down. I noticed the window was up; so he had clumb in by the shed. He kept a-looking me all over. By and by he says:

"Starchy clothes—very. You think you're a good deal of a big-bug, *don't* you?"

"Maybe I am, maybe I ain't," I says.

✍ DRILL #4 ✍

Now answer the following questions about the passage.

1. How old is Huck Finn's father?

2. What is he wearing?

3. What two things does Huck compare his father's complexion to?

4. Judging by how he uses it, what do you think Huck means by the word "tanned"?

5. What kind of relationship does Huck have with his father?

The answers can be found on page 171.

Chapter Four Glossary

bellow (bĕl′ ō) (v.) to make a loud, deep, hollow sound

lapse (lăps) (v.) to sink or slip gradually

maul (môl) (v.) injure by beating or tearing; bruise or lacerate

ruffled (ruf′ əld) (adj.) uneven, wrinkled, disturbed, irritated

Chapter 5
Detour to Boston

No sense wasting time, as my Aunt Alma May used to say before she had to undertake some unpleasant task. She was a sensible calico, Aunt Alma. A pillar of strength among the previous generation's litter. So with her words ringing in my ears, I approached the fireplace to begin another trip. Plunging into the pitch dark with its howling, mournful wind was a lot harder the second time, as now I knew what was waiting inside that fireplace: a seemingly endless fall, a disorienting lack of knowledge about which way was up, and a rather hard landing when we reached the bottom.

To take my mind off this unavoidably painful fate, I **indulged** in a little **reminiscence** regarding a house I once lived in on the Chesapeake Bay. As luck would have it, the house was just down the way from an oyster canning factory, and I managed to become friendly with the factory owner's cat, a remarkable blue-eyed Persian named Rayette. Now, while Rayette was rather far along in years, she retained a lively sense of mischief that in no way decreased her supply of ladylike grace. Once I managed to gain her trust (a feat that, if I may say so, took me less than the sum total of an afternoon), Rayette showed me to the shucking room of her owner's enormous and forbidding factory. There, I assumed, is where the dear girl had acquired her ample but by no means indelicate proportions. As agreed to beforehand, I met Rayette at the back door of the factory at midnight one night, and she showed me where a pane of glass in one of the windows on the second floor had been broken and left unrepaired. I followed Rayette up the rusted iron outer staircase, jumped to the railing, and crawled along the ledge to the window in question. Stealing a glance out over the dark calmness of the bay, I had a brief sensation of uneasiness, as if what I was about to do should not be done. Shaking it off, I ducked into the factory.

Alas! One should trust one's **intuition**! We had only just tipped over a barrel of shucked oysters and begun to dine when the shucking room lights were turned on with a violent snap and a huge, angry man with hobnailed boots came charging toward us, yelling, "Rayette! So it's you! My own cat, eating my profits! And with a **mongrel**! I'll show you!"

A mongrel, he called me! Mongrel indeed! I turned to Rayette to ask her to please reason with this monster, but she was gone. My lovely Rayette had fled without so much as a passing interest in my welfare. But there was no time to be **disillusioned**. Her owner was swinging his cane at me. I dodged several attempted blows, until the unhealthy-looking brute was fairly well tuckered out, then made my escape. Not long after that episode, I was forced to quit town entirely, as the oyster canning tycoon had paid a visit to the family I was staying with, who were his neighbors. I am afraid that the family, though they had shown me no ill will up to that point, took his side completely and there was talk of absolutely **barbaric** punishments. It was all for the best, though, because my forced travels took me north, to the Midwest, where I was able to establish residence on a series of farms and meet some lively companions. Now, let me see, what were their names? There was LeAnn, and there was Bobbie Sue, and—oh! How could I forget—

Of all the times to hit the bottom. I was forced to abandon my reminiscence, struggle off of my back, and scramble out of the way of the falling youngsters. But no matter how I scrambled I couldn't seem to go anywhere. The surface was slippery and cold. I was still trying mightily to run when Bridget fell on and nearly flattened me. Thank goodness she is on the small side. Unfortunately, Babette and Barnaby were right behind her.

✎ ✎ ✎ ✎ ✎

"Let me up!" Barnaby howled. "I'm getting back to my lab right away!" The young scientist pushed Babette off of him, stood up, and promptly fell down again. He stood up again, and this time his feet slipped out from under him completely and he fell hard on his rear end. "Ow," he said in a small voice, completely **bewildered**. "What's going on?"

Bridget, still on all fours, looked around. The kids were sprawled in the middle of a wide expanse of snowy ice. Snow was falling gently from the sky and coating the tall evergreen trees nearby. Bridget also saw a couple of small houses with smoke rising from the chimneys.

"I don't think we're in New York yet, Barnaby," she said.

"Well, then," Barnaby replied, "where are we?"

"It is a frozen lake, I think," Babette said, managing to stand upright without looking as though she was trying hard to keep from slipping.

"But that's crazy!" Barnaby insisted. "It's only September!" He wobbled carefully to his feet. Bridget did the same.

"Not here it isn't," Bridget said, squinting into the glare. She spotted a couple of teenagers stepping onto the ice with skates on their feet. It was a boy and a girl, and though they were kind of far away, Bridget could see that they were strangely dressed. The boy was wearing a fur hat, for one thing, and a fancy overcoat, and the girl had on a long, cloth coat, fitted at the waist. The hem of an ankle-length dress peeked out from the bottom of the coat and brushed the tops of her skates.

"Uh oh," Bridget said. "I was afraid of this."

"Afraid of what?" Barnaby demanded, shivering suddenly. "What were you afraid of?"

"Well," Bridget answered. "Not only aren't we back in New York, but I don't think we even made it back to the real world."

"We are in another book?" Babette inquired.

"I think so," Bridget told her.

"Wonderful!" Barnaby shrieked, flailing his arms. He should have expressed himself another way, because the flailing of his arms upset his balance and sent him sprawling on his back again. He sat on the ice and rubbed his elbow dejectedly. "We're never gonna get home."

"Calm down, Barnaby," Bridget said. "I don't like it any more than you do, but we have to deal with it. Who knows? While we're here we might find another way to stop Fence. Maybe these kids can help us." She raised her arms over her head and waved them back and forth, gently though, to avoid falling. "Hey!" she yelled. "Over here!"

The two teenagers, who had been racing each other and were apparently engaged in a playful dispute over who the winner was, stopped and turned at the sound of Bridget's voice. The four friends saw them look at each other and then skate speedily toward them.

"What ho!" the boy said when he skidded to a stop in front of them.

"Has anyone been hurt?" the girl who was with him asked. They both smiled cheerfully, but still managed to seem concerned.

"Not really," Bridget said.

"But you haven't any skates on, the lot of you," the boy noted. "Whatever are you doing out here?"

"Um . . ." Bridget began.

"Laurie!" the girl in the dress cut in. "I **beseech** you not to stick your less than spotless nose where it does not belong. These people seem to be in some distress. Think of offering them assistance, not how they came to be here!"

The boy in the funny Russian-looking hat and fancy overcoat looked apologetic. He bowed, first to Bridget and then to the others. "One thousand apologies, good people," he said. "How may we assist you?"

"Um . . ." said Bridget, shivering. She looked around at her friends, who were hugging themselves. Beauregard was walking around in circles, pausing after each step to hold one front and one back paw off of the ice, so that only two paws would be freezing at a time.

"Right now I guess we need a place to get warm," Bridget said.

"But of course!" the girl exclaimed. "You all look as though you're frozen solid. I shan't inquire as to how you came to be in the middle of the lake without warm clothes, for that would make me guilty of the same crime as my **boorish** companion."

"I have already begged pardon, as a gentleman should," the boy called Laurie complained.

"And you're forgiven," his friend replied. "I was only having you on. But as you mentioned gentlemanliness, perhaps you might offer one of these young ladies your greatcoat. And I shall do the same." The girl took off her coat and Laurie followed suit. Bridget and Babette tried to refuse, but the two skaters wouldn't hear of it. They insisted that their coats be borrowed for the walk to the house. Bridget and Babette put the coats on. Babette took Laurie's coat, which was only a little bit too long for her, but the girl was tall, and her coat hung in folds around Bridget's feet. Still, she was glad to have it. For good measure, Laurie removed his big fur hat and clapped it down on Barnaby's head.

Barnaby was tongue-tied. "Uh . . . th-thanks," he stammered, either because of nervousness or because of the cold.

"'Tis nothing, good fellow!" Laurie cried heartily.

The girl said, "Come away to our **hearthside**! We shall have you all warmed up in a **trice**!" And with that she turned and skated toward the edge of the lake, Laurie just behind her. Bridget, Barnaby, Babette, and Beauregard wobbled and skidded after them as best they could.

The house was not far from the lake, and when they got to it, the traveling friends were arranged in front of the fire with blankets wrapped around three of them and the fourth curled up on the floor just a foot or two from the roaring blaze.

The girl had a laugh at Beauregard's size and talent for instant relaxation. "I say! My sister, Beth, would melt at the sight of him. She is sort of the sworn protector of kittens and injured dolls. Laurie! Go summon Beth!"

Laurie went upstairs.

"We can't thank you enough for helping us out," Bridget said.

"We are so grateful," Babette added.

The girl waved their thanks away with a quick gesture of her hand. "It is not any hardship for us," the girl said. "We are desperate to be of service. Marmee always tells us—but wait, how rude of me! I haven't asked any of your names, nor have I told you mine. I am Josephine March, but I prefer to be called Jo. And what are you called?"

Bridget introduced herself and her friends.

"What adorable names you have. I wish I had any one of them instead of what I've got. But, oh well."

"Please excuse me for asking," Bridget said. Jo's **emphasis** on manners was making her self-conscious. Bridget rarely, if ever, excused herself before asking a question. "But can you give us an idea of where we are?"

Jo paused for only a moment, and then, as though it wasn't an odd question, she answered, "Why, you are in Massachusetts, near the city of Boston. This is the March household. Father is away, a chaplain in the army, and Mother is visiting him in the hospital, where he is ill but mending."

"When does Meg come home?" Babette suddenly piped up. Jo started and stared, for she had not yet mentioned her sister Meg.

"What a pretty cat," a soft voice exclaimed. Everyone turned to see a younger version of Jo coming down to the foot of the stairs. She turned her gaze from Beauregard to the group, then shifted it shyly to the floor. "Who does he belong to?"

"Um," Bridget said, "he sort of belongs to himself."

"Would he mind terribly if I petted him?" the young girl asked, still not looking up.

"Not at all."

The girl walked over to where Beauregard was lying and stroked his shiny, black fur, speaking to him softly. Beauregard stretched a little but didn't open his eyes.

"Beth," Jo said, "these are our new friends, Bridget, Babette— Babette! It's lovely—and Barnaby. Friends, this is my younger sister, Beth."

"Hi," the young travelers all said. Beth only partially looked up, but curtsied.

Jo got back down to business in a businesslike way. "So you say you know Meg, my older sister? May I ask where from?"

Bridget opened her mouth, but nothing came out. She didn't know whether to tell the whole truth, just some of it, or none at all.

Babette came to her rescue. "We have read in the newspaper about Meg's trip to Vanity Fair and the ball held at the house of the Moffats, her friends." Bridget looked at Babette, stunned. "When you have told us that this was the March household, I thought that Margaret March must be the same one as the news-paper said."

"Oh! Indeed?" Jo cried, delighted. "Where was it written about? We didn't even know! Wait until mother returns! She'll shout when she learns of it! Where did you say the article appeared?"

Babette hadn't said where the article appeared, because it hadn't appeared, and she was trying to think of the name of a newspaper, real or imaginary, where she could say she'd read about Meg.

Another blessed interruption occurred just then to spare Babette the trouble. A knock at the front door distracted Jo. "Who can that be? Laurie! Oh, where's he got to? I guess I'll check myself then. Please do excuse me, I'll just be a moment."

Jo got up and went into the next room to answer the door. Beth had led Beauregard upstairs, preferring to **commune** with him in greater privacy, and the three friends found themselves momentarily alone.

"Babette!" Bridget said in a loud whisper. "What was all that about Meg and some party? And how do you know about it?"

"Because I have read this book that we are in right now. It is *Little Women* by Louisa May Alcott, about the March family, who live in Massachusetts during your American Civil War. Did you not read it?"

"No," Bridget said. "But I've heard of it."

"That's funny," Babette said, cocking her head to one side. "I thought that all young girls read *Little Women*."

Bridget shook her head. "Too sappy for my taste," she said. "I'm more into mysteries."

"You should read it," Babette urged. "It is a beautiful story. And Jo is a lot like you, I think. A tomboy."

"She can read it when she gets home!" Barnaby butted in. "Right now let's get *out* of it. Let's go back to the lake. I'm not cold anymore. We can find our way back to the continuum."

"So this book takes place in the 1860s?" Bridget said, looking around.

"Yes," Babette said. "As we are traveling from book to book we are traveling forward in time. When we were in *The Adventures of Huckleberry Finn*, we were in the early nineteenth century. Now we are in the middle of the century."

Bridget got up and walked to the window, distractedly dropping her blanket on the floor. She looked out at the snow falling, the quiet street, the few houses nearby. A horse-drawn carriage glided by. "No cars," she said.

"No cars, no telephones, no television. No nothing!" Barnaby said. He was evidently upset.

Bridget turned away from the window. "Barnaby, shush!" she said. "Let's try not to freak out here."

"Let's go back to the lake now," Barnaby repeated. "Come on, it's still light. We can find where to get back to the continuum!"

Just take it easy," Bridget said. "Let me think."

"I should imagine that your capacity for thinking will be greatly enhanced by a good meal!" It was Jo, who had returned to the room. "Hannah, our family's cook, has returned from the shops and promised a hearty 'feed.' Nothing gourmet, but very satisfying. You will stay for dinner, won't you?"

None of the friends could say no, although Barnaby would have liked to.

"Good!" Jo said. "And after dinner, my sisters and I can perform for you! We've been rehearsing a play for a **fortnight**. Just a **trifle** I wrote. Would you care to see it?"

"You're a writer?" Bridget said.

"Heavens, no!" Jo laughed. "Just a scribbler of no account whatsoever. But I hope to be a writer someday. I *do* try. And my dear sisters are ever such delightful actresses. But if Meg, who you've read about—I must tell her of her stardom!—and my youngest sister Amy don't appear soon, we may have to recruit actors from the audience. Have any of you three ever performed?"

Bridget, Babette, and Barnaby all shook their heads.

"Oh but it's such great fun! Barnaby, usually we don't admit gentlemen into the theater, but perhaps I could **induce** you to play the male lead."

Barnaby looked stricken. He stammered out a polite refusal.

"Barnaby's a scientist, not an actor," Bridget said.

"I could tell by his smart chemist's tunic!" Jo said. "Okay then, Barnaby. I'll play the male lead myself. It's my wont anyway." They heard the front door open and shut. "That must be Meg! We must get started on the set!" Jo leapt up and went to meet Meg, entirely forgetting to ask again where Babette had read about Meg's debut.

"Tunic?" Barnaby said, dazed by Jo's vibrant personality. "I don't wear a tunic."

Babette looked at Barnaby's lab coat. "It is *like* a tunic."

"It is not!" Barnaby insisted.

At dinner, the four sisters—Meg and Amy had **straggled** in and been introduced—talked among themselves about the play they were to perform (a musical drama about an enchanted kingdom), the letters they had each received from their mother, and various other things. Bridget, Barnaby, and Babette managed to say very little about themselves, responding to the sisters' polite questions about where they were from and what their hometowns were like.

"I should love to visit Paris some day!" Amy, the youngest March sister, exclaimed. She seemed fascinated by Babette's sunglasses and insisted on wearing them. Babette handed them over, squinting, even though it wasn't very bright in the dining room. Meg, the oldest and most formal of the sisters, made Amy give the sunglasses back.

In Jo's play, a villainous count sought to enlist the help of a witch to foil two young lovers. There was singing; there were costumes; there was a tall plywood tower where the heroine sat in the window, **serenaded** by the hero. Bridget, Babette, and Barnaby sat in the Marches' living room and watched the romantic tale unfold. It was a good play, all in all, despite some flubbed lines and eccentric costumes (Jo wore the same boots to play both villain and hero). But in the middle of act three the performance was rudely interrupted by a loud, insistent knock at the front door. Everyone, performers and audience members alike, turned toward the kitchen.

"Keep going!" Jo told her sisters in a loud whisper. "Hannah will answer the door!" She turned to the three friends. "Please keep your seats! This is the turning point coming up!"

But just then, the buzz of the quarreling voices in the kitchen reached a **crescendo**. A moment later, Hannah rushed into the living room, followed by a large man with a mustache and enormous side-whiskers, accompanied by two constables. The first man entered the room and stood still a moment, looking at each person there.

"Excuse me, ladies," he said. "Sorry to barge in. I'm Bertram Rawlins, chief of police of the city of Boston, and I need a word with . . ." The chief paused and his gaze came to rest on Barnaby, "with you, sir."

The man walked over to where Barnaby was sitting and stood before him. Barnaby cowered on the sofa.

"M–m–me?" he said in a small, frightened voice.

"Yes, sir," the chief replied. "See, we got a tip that there was a Confederate spy in our midst, and you answer the description."

"Spy!" Jo and Bridget cried in unison, Jo ripping off her hat and Bridget jumping up from the sofa.

"But he's only fourteen years old!" Bridget reasoned.

The police chief shook his head. "That's no defense, miss. Everyone knows that the rebel army's out-numbered, and that its commanders press young boys into service on the battlefield. So it only follows that they would use teenagers as spies, too." He turned back to Barnaby. "Sir," the chief said. "I must ask that you submit to a search."

"Um . . . okay," Barnaby said. The two constables searched the trembling young scientist. The March sisters stood by in their costumes and watched.

"He hasn't any **communiqués** or strategic plans on him, sir," the first constable said to the chief when they were finished. "He's just got this strange device." The constable held up the ionic fibrillator's remote control.

The chief took the brass wand and turned it over in his hands, looking at it and frowning. He shifted his gaze to Barnaby, who flinched.

"So what do you call this?" the forbidding man finally asked. "Is it a weapon of some kind?"

Barnaby took a moment to find his voice. "N–no!" he said. "It's just something—something from an experiment I was doing back home."

"And where would that be?"

"New York City!" Bridget interjected.

The police chief turned and looked down at Bridget, who stood her ground.

"Excuse me, dear girl," the chief said, "but I b'lieve the young gentleman can answer my questions on his own." The chief turned back to Barnaby. "So you hail from New York City, eh? How'd you get here?"

Barnaby was stumped by that one. He looked at Bridget for some help. She looked at the floor and shook her head, knowing his looking at her was a mistake.

"Don't know the answer?" Police Chief Rawlins said. "Maybe a trip down to the station house will refresh your memory. You'd better come too, young lady," he said to Bridget. I'd like to know how you're mixed up in this boy's business." He nodded to the two constables. One grabbed Barnaby, the other Bridget.

"But you can't just arrest them!" Jo insisted. "You have no evidence that they've done anything wrong!"

"Now, with all respect, miss," Chief Rawlins said, "we got a tip from an informant and, being wartime, we've got to investigate as thoroughly as we can. Come on, boys." And, with that, the three policemen led Bridget and Barnaby out of the house to a waiting carriage. Night had fallen, and Babette thought her friends looked heartbreakingly vulnerable as she watched them being put in the carriage by the policemen in the old-fashioned uniforms.

"This is an outrage!" Jo cried. "Imagine guests of ours being treated so! I am most dreadfully embarrassed."

Meg, the eldest sister, spoke then, in a soft voice to cool Jo down. "Chief Rawlins is simply mistaken," she said, "but is taking every precaution, as well he should. I am sure our friends will be released by morning."

Jo turned on her sister, furious. "'As well he should!'" she repeated. "Why, what a traitor you are! I suppose he should be allowed to just barge into people's houses and drag them away on the basis of 'tips'? Perhaps I should send a note to the good chief, reporting the dangerous activities of a certain Margaret March!"

"Now, Jo, don't exaggerate," Meg scolded. "What if there should be a spy in our midst? It is not so unbelievable. After all, we take strangers into our home with **nary** a thought as to their origins. And we know so little about them. Like Babette there." Meg inclined her head toward Babette, who was sitting on the sofa, and curtsied slightly. "She is very nice, to be sure, but what do we really know about her?"

Little Amy, who was particularly fond of Babette, interjected. "Now you leave Babette alone! She is so nice and solifitous she even remembered the writing about you going to the Moffats' party in the newspaper."

Meg was about to giggle at Amy's mispronunciation of the word **solicitous** but she stopped and frowned. "But the party hasn't been written about," she said.

"But Babette read about it," Jo insisted. "She told us! In the . . . where was it?" Jo turned to Babette, who sat, expressionless, on the sofa. Meg and Amy turned to look at her too.

"I should like to know, as well," Meg said. "For the ball was only last week. None of the weekly journals have published since then and the daily newspapers have not mentioned it."

The three March sisters looked inquiringly at Babette, who sighed. She knew she was going to have to come clean.

✎ ✎ ✎ ✎ ✎

The cell had a hard bench, a stone floor, and nothing else. This night, Bridget and Barnaby were the police department's only prisoners.

Bridget leaned against the bars of the cell while Barnaby sat hunched over on the bench, moaning. "What now?" he said. "Arrested for spying! I'll lose my grant, that's what now. Dean O'Malley will never let me continue at the university! If I ever get back home, that is. They'll probably put me in the stocks for this here!"

"Relax, Barnaby," Bridget said. "This is the nineteenth century. They don't put people in stocks here. Now, if this book was set in the seventeenth century, like *The Scarlet Letter*, or something like that, I'd say go ahead and worry."

"Well," Barnaby replied. "How about hanging? Don't they hang spies?"

Bridget thought about it. She turned away from the bars and looked at Barnaby. "You're right," she said. "I guess they might hang you."

Barnaby groaned.

"But we're not going to let them do that," Bridget continued hurriedly. "There has to be a way out of this. I've just got to think." She walked to the little window high up on the wall at the back of her cell, jumping up on the bench to look out through the bars into the snowy night. A carriage rolled by and a few heavily bundled people trudged through the snow under the gas street lamp on the corner.

"Who could have framed you?" Bridget asked, hitting one of the hard, cold iron bars with her fist. "It doesn't make any sense."

"What does it matter?" Barnaby asked. "Stuck here we can't get back to the lake and back home. And when we get everything cleared up, it'll be too late to stop Fence."

Bridget jumped down and sat next to Barnaby on the bench, kicking her legs back and forth in her frustration. "Babette will come through somehow," Bridget asserted. "I know she will."

Bridget kicked her legs some more and fished out a fresh piece of chewing gum, stuffing it into her mouth with the others. Barnaby moaned some more. The wind whistled through the corridor and echoed eerily in the empty cells.

Then something happened that made the two friends look at each other: They heard a faint thump on the wall behind them. Then they heard another thump. "What the . . ." Bridget began, standing up and turning to look at the high window. As she turned, a snowball flew in and hit her in the head, knocking her Yankees cap off.

"Hey!" Bridget said. Barnaby looked up at the window then too. "There's somebody out there!"

Bridget jumped up on the bench and looked out. Jo, Laurie, Babette, and Beauregard were under the window in the moonlight. They had brought a carriage and horses.

"Jo! Thank goodness you're here!" Bridget said.

"Shh!" Jo put a finger to her lips. "We haven't time to talk. Take this rope and tie it to the bars." Jo threw the end of a rope up to the window. Bridget caught it and tied it securely around the bars. The other end was already fastened to the back of the carriage. Laurie jumped up on the coach seat and gave a little flick of his whip to the horses. The animals leapt forward, causing the rope to tighten and vibrate with tension. Laurie flicked the whip again, and the horses strained mightily in the snow. The kids could hear a slight crunching noise as the concrete wall began to give way.

"Duck, Babette!" Jo yelled. Babette did. With a crash, the bars popped out of the window, taking some concrete and brick with them and leaving a jagged hole.

"Yay!" Bridget and Barnaby yelled, hugging each other.

"Hey!" a voice behind them shouted. They turned to see the guard rushing up to the cell, fumbling with a ring of keys, a look of disbelief on his face.

"Come on!" Jo yelled. Bridget went out the window first, followed by Barnaby. The guard gave up fumbling with the keys and ran into the other room to sound the alarm.

Outside the kids piled into the carriage while Laurie jumped down and cut the rope loose from the back. "You saved us!" Bridget said to Jo.

"Do not thank us yet!" Jo cried, all smiles.

Laurie leapt up onto the top of the carriage and whipped the horses into action. In a moment, they were flying down the road out of town with the police still stuck back at the station hitching their horses up to their wagon.

"My remote!" Barnaby said. "The ionic fibrillator! The police confiscated it!"

"Will you forget about that dumb fibrillator, Barnaby!" Bridget yelled.

"Do not worry," Babette told Barnaby. "Beauregard went to get it."

In a flash, Beauregard tore out of the station house and up the road after the kids' carriage, overtaking the wagon full of policemen, which had finally gotten underway. As he drew up alongside Laurie's carriage, Babette caught sight of him, his big, black paws tearing at the snow, the fibrillator's remote clutched in his teeth.

"There he is!" Babette shouted. Beauregard leapt to the running board, and Jo opened the door of the carriage to let him hop in just as Laurie took a sharp curve in the road. The back wheels of the carriage skidded on the packed snow.

"Whoa!" Barnaby exclaimed. The kids tumbled all over the inside of the carriage. The momentum of the skid threw Beauregard off the running board, forcing him to dig his claws into the canvas top of the carriage and slamming his body against the opened door. When the carriage righted itself, Jo grabbed Beauregard and pulled him inside.

"All right, Beauregard!" Bridget yelled, hugging the big cat to her. Beauregard spat the remote control onto Barnaby's lap and shook himself all over.

All the kids braced themselves, for the carriage was traveling so quickly it felt like it could go out of control again at any moment. Through the small back window, they could see the police wagon, with its four-horse team, still in hot pursuit. As Laurie took another curve, Bridget looked out the side window and saw the frozen expanse of the lake coming into view. She turned to Jo and took her by the arm.

"Listen, Jo," she said. "Let us out here. We have to get to the middle of the lake. I can't really explain it."

"But Babette already has!" Jo exclaimed. "Your mission is so noble! This villainous tyrant must be stopped. I only wish I could join you on your quest. But, alas, I must stay and tend the hearth fire, as they say. I'll tell Laurie to stop the carriage and let you out."

"Wait!" Bridget stopped her. "I'd hate for you to get caught," she said. "Let us climb up to the top of the carriage. I have a way to get to the lake by air."

"By air?" Jo repeated. "How on earth . . ."

"Trust me," Bridget replied. "It's my specialty."

As the carriage sped along beside the lake, Bridget turned her cap backwards on her head and climbed out the door and up the side of the coach, followed by Babette, Barnaby, and Beauregard. The wind tugged at their clothes and raked their faces; the carriage bounced and jolted along the bumpy road as though trying to buck them off; but they all made it.

"Hold on to me!" Bridget yelled over the wind. Each of her friends grabbed a limb. Then Bridget began to blow a bubble with the gum in her mouth. After a few misses, she finally succeeded, blowing it bigger and bigger, until the bubble was larger than all four of them put together, and the wind started to catch it. Suddenly, they lifted off the roof of the carriage and floated up into the air. Babette, clutching Bridget's left leg for dear life, looked down and saw the carriage turn off toward the house. The police wagon pulled to a stop. They were still low enough for her to see the astonished faces of the policemen in the wagon. Barnaby couldn't share her satisfaction at seeing this. His eyes were shut tight.

The kids floated up to the treetops and out over the lake, the snow-crusted ice aglow beneath them.

"We are almost over the center!" Babette shouted.

But, just then the bubble, brittle from the cold air, burst. The kids and cat plummeted to the ice and lay in a heap, dusted by specks of snow. Barnaby opened his eyes. At the edge of the lake, about fifty yards away, Police Chief Rawlins and several policemen were stepping gingerly onto the ice. The policemen were carrying nightsticks.

"Let's get to that hole in the ice quick!" Barnaby said. He tried to get up, but slipped. The girls were having the same problem.

Beauregard, however, had gotten up and dug his claws into the ice. He was standing up perfectly steadily. He flicked his tail at Bridget, who grabbed a hold of it.

"Guys!" Bridget said. "Grab my feet!" Babette gabbed Bridget's feet and Barnaby grabbed Babette's.

"Go, Beauregard!" Bridget yelled. "Here come the cops!"

Beauregard took off, his claws digging into the ice. He pulled the chain of young humans along behind him like a long wriggling worm. Chief Rawlins yelled at them not to go near the center of the lake, where the ice was thin.

"Come back, children!" he bellowed. "You'll get a fair trial!" But the wind drowned out his voice.

When Beauregard reached the hole in the center of the lake, he leapt straight into it, with Bridget still holding onto his tail and, Babette and Barnaby streaming into the hole behind them.

In *Little Women*, Louisa May Alcott based the Marches on her own family, although she changed a lot of the details. Jo is patterned after Louisa herself, who shared with her main character her passion for reading and her quick temper.

Read the following passage from the book and then try to answer the questions that follow it:

> Beth was too bashful to go to school; it had been tried, but she suffered so much that it was given up, and she did her lessons at home, with her father. Even when he went away, and her mother was called to devote her skill and energy to Soldiers' Aid Societies, Beth went faithfully on by herself, and did the best she could. She was a housewifely little creature, and helped Hannah keep home neat and comfortable for the workers, never thinking of any reward but to be loved. Long, quiet days she spent, not lonely nor idle, for her little world was peopled by imaginary friends, and she was by nature a busy bee. There were six dolls to be taken up and dressed every morning, for Beth was

a child still, and loved her pets as well as ever; not one whole or handsome one among them; all were outcasts till Beth took them in; for, when her sisters outgrew these idols, they passed to her, because Amy would have nothing old or ugly. Beth cherished them all the more tenderly for that very reason, and set up a hospital for infirm dolls. No pins were ever stuck into their cotton vitals; no harsh words or blows were ever given them; no neglect ever saddened the heart of the most repulsive, but all were fed and clothed, nursed and caressed, with an affection which never failed.

✍ DRILL #5 ✍

Answer the following questions. Consider the information in the chapter as well as that in the paragraph.

1. Why is Beth's father away?
   a. He's a chaplain in the army.
   b. He's a ship's captain at sea.
   c. He's a traveling salesman.

2. Who is the youngest March sister, Beth or Amy?

3. Why does Beth get all the dolls her sisters discard and not Amy?
   a. Beth is selfish.
   b. Amy's sisters don't like her.
   c. Amy doesn't like old dolls.

4. Why is Beth taught at home instead of in school?
   a. Girls didn't go to school back then.
   b. Beth's parents don't believe in school.
   c. Beth is painfully shy.

5. How many dolls does Beth care for in her "hospital"?

   a. 14

   b. 6

   c. 8

Chapter Five Glossary

ample (am′ pəl) (adj.) large in size; spacious; roomy; more than enough; abundant

barbaric (bär-băr′ ĭk) (adj.) characteristic of barbarians; uncivilized; primitive; unrestrained

beseech (bĭ-sēch′) (v.) ask earnestly and eagerly; beg

bewildered (bĭ-wil′ dər) (adj.) hopelessly confused; puzzled

boorish (boŏr′ ish) (adj.) rude; awkward; ill-mannered

commune (kə-myōōn′) (v.) talk together intimately

communiqué (kə-myōō′nĭ-kā′) (n.) an official communication or bulletin

crescendo (krə-shĕn′ dō) (n.) a gradual increase in loudness

disillusioned (dis′ ĭ-lōō′ zhənd) (adj.) disappointed; bitter; stripped of ideals

disorienting (dĭs-or′ e-ent′ āting) (adj.) causing to lose one's bearings; causing confusion

emphasis (em′ fə-sis) (n.) special attention given to something to make it stand out; importance; stress; weight

fortnight (fôrt′ nĭt′) (n.) a period of two weeks

hearthside (härth′ sĭd′) (n.) fireside

induce (ĭn-dōōs′) (v.) lead on to some action or belief; persuade

indulge (ĭn-dŭlj′) (v.) give way to one's own desires

intuition (ĭn-tōō-ĭsh′ ən) (n.) the direct knowing or learning of something without the conscious use of reasoning; immediate apprehension or understanding

mournful (môrn′ fəl) (adj.) characterized by mourning; sorrowful; causing sorrow or depression; melancholy

nary (nâr′ ē) (adj.) not any; no

pillar (pĭl′ ər) (n.) a person who is the main support of an institution or group

reminiscence (rem′ ə-nĭs′ əns) (n.) the act of remembering or recollecting past experiences; a memory or recollection

serenade (sĕr′ ə-nād′) (v.) to perform for a lover by singing or playing an instrument outdoors in the evening

solicitous (sə-lĭs′ ĭ-təs) (adj.) showing care, attention, or concern

straggle (străg′ əl) (v.) leave, arrive, or occur at irregular intervals

trice (trĭs) (n.) a very short time; an instant; a moment

trifle (trī′ fəl) (n.) somthing of little value or importance

tunic (tōō′ nĭk) (n.) a blouse-like garment extending to the hips or lower, usually gathered at the waist, often with a belt

vibrant (vī′ brənt) (adj.) vigorous, energetic, radiant, sparkling, vivacious, etc.

Chapter 6
Merry Old England

Catching up to that carriage was quite a feat, I must say, although hardly a spectacular one for me. My human acquaintances find it hard to believe that I'm so athletic. They are limited by the shallow observations they have made concerning my sleeping habits and my appetite. But I am really much more active than they believe, and strive to achieve balance among my few, middling vices and my strenuous physical regimen.

How do I remain in such Olympic trim? It's a feline secret known to only a very few of the lesser species. Perhaps running through a typical day in my life would help to illustrate my point.

I awake a couple of hours before sunset (a nocturnal schedule is vital to one's well-being) and stretch. Then I go in search of breakfast. After a post meal bath, I have a doze. Getting up refreshed, I find a small ball or a bottle cap (anything light and **aerodynamic** will do) and bat it around for a few minutes to warm up. This sharpens paw-eye coordination and quickens the footwork, much as skipping rope trains a boxer to move more swiftly about the ring, thereby evading his opponent's blows.

After the preliminary workout, I rest for awhile and contemplate my surroundings. If I am in the country, there will be any number of small animals to chase, providing me with both exercise and my next (low-fat) meal. New York City apartments, however, generally offer only two varieties of **adversary**, insects and mice. But one must work with what one has.

Of course, when staying in the city, one expects to be provided with food by one's hosts, so that the insects and mice become mere playthings. This is where the feline concept of balance comes in. Cats don't eat much at each meal, but we have many more than three meals per day. Even when food is set out for us, we tend to visit our bowls on numerous occasions between dusk and dawn, snacking rather than really digging in. Of course, many cats of a certain age show the signs of overindulgence nonetheless, but these tend to be cats who have forgotten the value of a small ball or a bottle cap. They have dismissed as the folly of youth the chasing down of animals smaller than oneself. These are cats who are too pampered by their human keepers. These are cats who are running grave health risks and require a stern talking to. These are cats who need to have smaller portions of food set out only at certain times of day.

Anyway, after I have surveyed my surroundings, and if I have found that there are no actual creatures to run after, I can opt for either chasing my own tail (absolute privacy is required for this maneuver), or running laps back and forth across the yard or apartment. After a brief nap, I repeat the process, eat some more food, and finally retire to a secluded spot to think over the mysteries of life and wait for bedtime.

Thus have I managed to preserve my **physique** and my kittenish demeanor—

Uh-oh! Here we go again.

✎ ✎ ✎ ✎ ✎

The four friends had hardly absorbed the painful **chafing** of the rough ice when they found themselves falling through darkness again and brought up short in a painfully tangled heap on a stone floor. They disentangled themselves and looked around. They were in some kind of chamber with a sloped roof. There were four windows, through which the kids could see bits of slate-gray sky. Above their heads was a network of huge gears, turning slowly.

"Ugh," Barnaby moaned. "Where are we?"

"I don't know," Bridget said.

Babette stood up, cracked her back, and straightened her sunglasses. "It looks like a clock tower."

Just then a deafening noise rang out above their heads, jarring the young adventurers out of their quiet **wonderment**. It was a bell, extremely close by, ringing the hour. The bell, which must have been enormous, rang three long **peals**, driving the kids to clap their hands over their ears and grimace in pain. Beauregard hopped around as though he wanted to run away but didn't know in what direction.

Finally, it was over, and everybody sank back to the floor, cradling their aching heads in their arms.

"I guess that would make it three o'clock," Barnaby said between clenched teeth.

"You're right," Babette said. "But what year?" She stood back up again and walked to one of the little windows. Peering out, she said, "Bridget! Come quickly!"

"I can't come quickly," Bridget reminded her. "I just fell on my back out of a continuum for the second time today." Bridget ambled slowly and creakily over to the window Babette was intently looking out of.

"We're in England," Babette told her.

"I'm not a bit surprised," Bridget answered.

Babette pointed as she spoke. "Look! There's London Bridge, and the House of Parliament."

Bridget looked. The people crossing the bridge on foot looked like ants. The traffic didn't include any automobiles, just carriages.

"Still no cars!" Bridget exclaimed. "Why can't we at least get into a book that takes place in our own century?"

"I have a better question!" Barnaby was upright now, and pacing back and forth, his eyes wild behind his spectacles. "Why can't we get home? That old coot said if we returned to where we entered the book, we'd get home. Not to another book! Home!"

The girls ignored Barnaby and continued to survey the scene from the clock tower.

"So," Bridget said, "if that's Parliament right down there, then this must be the Parliament clock tower."

"Yes," Babette replied. "The bell and the clock are called 'Big Ben.'"

Bridget nodded. "I know," she said. "I've been here before, with my parents."

The two girls turned away from the window.

"So," Babette began. "What book do you think we're in?"

"There's only one way to find out," Bridget said, smiling. She was beginning to get into the whole thing. "Walk the streets until we stumble onto a plot or something."

"Let's go," her friend said.

"Barnaby! Beauregard! We're off!"

After a long climb down a very steep flight of stairs, the young adventurers found themselves on the streets of London, not sure which way to go. Bridget finally chose a way, and they all walked along in the gray afternoon, looking at the unfamiliar sights. They walked down muddy, cobblestone streets, past storefronts and taverns, over London Bridge, through Piccadilly Circus, and by row houses and stables. They came to an open-air market where huge cuts of meat were sold on long wooden tables, alongside sellers of scrap metal and hats and handkerchiefs. The streets **teemed** with horses and carriages and the gutters were piled high with horse manure.

"Not a very clean city," Bridget sniffed. "Even by New York standards."

"New York probably looked a lot like this in the early nineteenth century," Babette told her, "which is where I think we have found our way back to."

"So we're not moving forward in time?" Barnaby said.

"I don't think it matters that much, Barnaby," Bridget said. "Every time we enter the continuum we have a chance to go to a book that takes place in the future."

"Or the past!" the scientist exploded. "We're going to end up in Dante's *Inferno*, or *The Iliad*, in the middle of the Trojan War! What then?" They all stopped short in the middle of the market crowd as Bridget and Barnaby stared each other down. Babette and Beauregard retired **stealthily** to a butcher's table in the market nearby. The table was covered with various pieces of meat, each with the same peculiar scent.

"What would you like me to do about it?" Bridget asked Barnaby. "It's not my fault we keep falling into another book every time we try to go home!"

Barnaby shot right back: "But couldn't we step *right back in* to the Continuum and try *again* to get home instead of going on a wild goose chase every time we enter another book?"

"Well . . ." Bridget began. She hated when Barnaby was right. But she recovered herself well. "Look!" she said. "In case you've forgotten, we're on a mission to stop Fence from abridging every book ever written. Doesn't that mean anything to you?"

Barnaby looked down at the muddy cobblestones, ashamed but unshaken. "I just want to go home," he said.

"Fine," Bridget said. "I understand. I'm sorry I dragged you on this crazy hunt, anyway. You go back to Big Ben and find the Continuum. We'll meet you back in New York. Babette?"

Bridget looked around and saw Babette standing at the butcher's table, apparently checking out the **unsavory**-looking meat.

Bridget and Barnaby sidled up to her.

"Uh, Babette," Bridget said. "Are you actually thinking of buying and *eating* something here?"

Babette smiled, a little uncharacteristically. "*Mais non*! Of course not. I am still quite satisfied by the meal we have enjoyed at the March's."

"Then why are you standing here?" Barnaby asked.

"My friends," Babette said, still smiling, "please don't look around, but have you noticed we are being followed?"

Bridget and Barnaby froze, trying not to search the crowd for someone who might be watching them.

"How do you know?" Bridget asked, staring at the fat on a large slab of mutton.

"I do *not* know for certain," Babette admitted. "But there are two men who I have seen near Big Ben, on London Bridge, and again in Piccadilly Circus, and now they are shopping at this open-air market. And, like us, they do not really seem at home."

"What'll we do?" Bridget said. "How do we find out what they want?"

"Well," Babette said. "Either we wait for them to approach us or we can approach them." The French martial artist cracked her knuckles and looked at her friend.

"That's a tough decision," Bridget said. "They might be dangerous."

"No kidding!" Barnaby retorted. "I think you guys should come with me."

"Come with you where?" Babette asked.

At that moment, Barnaby was **jostled** by two grimy young boys in oversized coats and beaten up boots. "Pardon us, sir! Excuse me very much indeed, sir!" the boys squealed.

"That's quite all right!" Barnaby called after them as they hurried away. He turned back to Bridget and Babette. "Where do you think? Back to Big Ben. Back to the continuum. Hopefully, back to New York!" Barnaby patted his lab coat. "Now let's get out of this germ-ridden novel right away. That meat alone is . . ." He patted his lab coat some more. "Hey!" he yelled. "The remote's gone again! Those kids picked my pocket!"

"Come on!" Bridget said, running in the direction that the two boys had gone. "They can't have gotten far!" Bridget sprinted up the cobblestone street, breaking out of the crowd around the market, with Beauregard and the others right behind her. As she ran, Bridget kicked up a steady stream of mud, for the streets were very muddy. Beauregard got a face full running behind her and had to stop for a wash.

The four friends soon found, to their dismay, that many tiny little lanes broke off from the main road, and that the two boys could have run down any one of them. Bridget tried one and then another, peering into alleyways and over backyard gates, to no **avail**. The boys had vanished into one of the row houses.

The four friends were breathless. They stopped and rested on a stoop.

"Great, we lost them!" Bridget said as she peered along the narrow little lane up to the main road, where people were walking by. "Sorry about your remote, Barnaby."

"That's okay," Barnaby said.

"Bridget," Babette said softly. "I think we should take a walk around the block."

"Why?" Bridget asked. "I'm upset, but I'm not *that* upset."

"Trust me," Babette said. "I believe that those who are following us are waiting around the corner for our next move. Wouldn't you like to see what they look like?"

"Let's go," Bridget said.

As Babette, Bridget, Barnaby, and Beauregard approached the corner, Babette counseled the others in a low voice. "Turn right up here. And try to look normal. They are two men with glasses. One has a jacket."

Everyone held their breath as they neared the corner, uncertain of what was on the other side.

They turned the corner and each of the young friends glanced around in a **nonchalant** manner, as though they were merely taking in the sights. They spotted the two men standing in a doorway. Barnaby, trembling involuntarily, whispered, "Is that them?"

"Shhh!" Bridget whispered back.

The men were wearing 1990s clothing: One had on a suit jacket and was wearing blue jeans. The other had on a plaid shirt and khakis. Both wore glasses and sneakers. They pretended to be studying a street map when the four friends passed.

Turning at the next corner, Bridget stopped. "I have a hunch that they must be the guys who turned Barnaby in to the police chief in *Little Women!*" she said.

"Yes," Babette agreed.

"It must have been some sort of delaying tactic," Bridget said.

Barnaby shook his head. "But who would want to delay us," he asked. "Besides . . ."

"Fence!" Bridget cried. Babette clapped her hand over Bridget's mouth. They all looked down the street, but the two men weren't in sight. Bridget tore Babette's hand away and went on. "He must know we're on this mission and he wants to stop it."

"But how could he know about the Fiction–Reality Continuum?" Barnaby asked. "Professor Thorvaldson would never tell."

"Who knows?" Bridget said. "Maybe he bugged Thorvaldson's office. Or maybe Dean O'Malley told him!"

"Never!" Barnaby said.

"It doesn't matter how he knows," Babette said. "We must get what we need to stop him and leave as soon as we can."

"I'm with you," Barnaby said.

"Where do we start?" Bridget asked Babette.

"First, we must find those two pickpockets, which I think we can do by returning to the scene of their last crime."

The four friends walked back to the market and hung around the stalls, trying to catch a glimpse of the ruffians who had snatched Barnaby's fibrillator remote. They wandered in and out of the tables of old meat, rotten vegetables, and filthy rags. They were jostled by men and women alike and checked their jackets after each jostle, expecting to find something missing. But nothing was, and they caught no sight of the two little pickpockets, until—

"Stop thief!" a man cried. The four friends whirled around with a good portion of the rest of the crowd and saw the two young boys running back along the street, turning the corner even as several of the men in the crowd took off in pursuit.

"Come on!" Bridget yelled, and the kids ran after them too, Beauregard pulling out ahead of the whole crowd and disappearing around the corner after the pickpockets. As Bridget, Babette, and Barnaby turned the corner, they saw the men from the market crowd turn the next corner and stop, looking around. The pick-pockets were nowhere in sight.

"Weer'd dey git to?" one man asked.

"Agh, we lost 'em," another replied, disgustedly.

The men retreated to the marketplace and Bridget, Babette, and Barnaby were left standing in the dismal little lane by themselves.

"Where's Beauregard?" Barnaby asked.

They peered along the line of rundown row houses and presently Beauregard's head appeared around the doorjamb of one of them.

"There!" cried Bridget. "He's over there!"

The three kids ran up to the cat and Bridget patted his head.

"Nice work again," Bridget said. "This must be where the pickpockets are hiding out."

"*Pardonne-moi,*" Babette said, motioning for her friends to step aside so she could kick the door in. She went into her stance. Bridget did not step aside, though.

"Wait, Babette!" she said.

"What is wrong?" Babette asked.

"I've got a hunch about where we are," Bridget said. "And if I'm right we might not want to just barge in on these people."

"Where are we?" Barnaby asked. Babette relaxed her pose.

"If I'm not mistaken," Bridget said, "the boy who picked your pocket is named Jack Dawkins, or the Artful Dodger. And the other boy is Charlie Bates."

"And?" Babette said.

"Their mentor is a criminal named Fagin," Bridget continued, "who works with a huge psychopath named Bill Sikes."

"We're in Charles Dickens's *Oliver Twist*?" Barnaby guessed.

"That's what I think," Bridget said.

Barnaby turned to Babette. "She's right," he said. "We shouldn't barge in, especially if Bill Sikes is in there."

"I have never read this Dickens book," Babette said. "These criminals, they are ruthless?"

"Not above killing us," Barnaby said. "Exactly."

Bridget looked up at the dingy, two-story house, with its shuttered windows. "If I remember correctly," she said, "they'll be holding

Oliver prisoner on the second floor. There may be only one of them downstairs to deal with, or there may be six."

Babette thought a moment. "Bridget, how much bubble gum do you have?"

In an upstairs room of the house that the four friends were standing in front of, Oliver Twist was indeed imprisoned by his cruel masters, and was weeping bitterly on a straw floor mat. Since his birth in a workhouse, Oliver, who was an orphan, had been the victim of the most brutal mistreatment. The only kindness shown him in his whole life was during his brief stay at the home of a gentleman, Mr. Brownlow, who'd taken pity on him.

But now he'd been kidnapped once again by the evil criminal **syndicate** run by Fagin, and was in despair over his very survival, when he heard something hard pound against the locked wooden shutter that covered the window.

Oliver, small and very slight, kept alive by the criminals on the most meager **rations**, retreated to the corner of the room, away from the window. He cowered there, wondering what could be pounding so hard against a window two stories high.

Incredibly, on the fourth or fifth pound, a black-slippered foot splintered the shutter and stuck through the hole. Oliver stared at the foot, stunned out of his fear. The foot disappeared, then came through the shutter again, followed by the rest of a teenage girl, dressed all in black, with black sunglasses on. "Olivair?" she inquired.

The poor boy could hardly reply. "Yes?" he finally managed to say.

"We are here to free you," the girl said. Oliver hesitated as Babette motioned to him. "There is not a moment to lose!"

Oliver stood and went to the window. "But how shall I get to the ground?" he asked. "I'll surely fall and **dash** my brains out on the paving stones!"

"*Pas du tout*," the girl said, in a language Oliver didn't recognize. "Meet my friend, Bridget." At that the girl hoisted Oliver onto the windowsill and he beheld the strangest sight he'd ever seen: a girl in a dark blue cap, suspended in midair by a giant bubble **protruding** from her mouth.

Oliver looked at the first girl in disbelief, then back at the floating marvel, who held out her hand. Oliver was reaching for it when the door to the room burst open and an enormous, black-bearded man shouldered his way into the room. He was heavy-browed, weaving slightly, and smelled of alcohol. It was the criminal named Bill Sikes.

"Wot's the bloody ruckus all . . ." the man began. His eyes widened when he saw the kids at the window. Then they narrowed into vicious slits. "Why, I'll tear out your **gizzard**, ye varmint!" The huge man lunged and Babette shoved Oliver out of the window. Bridget caught his hand, and his small weight brought them gently down to the cobblestone street.

Up in the room, Babette was fighting off Bill Sikes. Evading a gigantic fist, she backhanded him across the face. Enraged, Sikes grabbed a hold of the slender girl and flung her all the way across the room. Hitting the wall, she landed on her feet and turned to face him. Then she heard a growl. A dirty dog with tan fur appeared at the top of the stairs and flashed his teeth.

"Sic 'er, boy!" Sikes commanded. "Do what yiz trained for!"

At his master's command, the dog lunged at Babette, who managed to get out of the way of its snapping jaws just in time. But the dog snapped again, got a hold of the toe of her left slipper, and pulled. Babette was caught off-balance and sank to a crouch. Sikes advanced.

"Ow'll teach you to meddle in my affairs," he growled.

Babette braced herself for a heavy blow.

But then she heard the quick patter of paws on the stairs. It was Beauregard! The big black cat zipped into the room in a flash and threw himself on the dog, who let go of Babette's slipper and yelped. Babette rolled across the floor, under Sikes' legs, and leapt into a standing position behind the **brutish felon**. Sikes wheeled around to face her and caught a kick flush against his chin.

He sat down hard. Then he fell sideways on the floor and rolled on his back, groaning.

With a ferocious swat and a high-pitched snarl, Beauregard dispatched the dog, who ran off whining all the way to his hiding place.

Babette and Beauregard hit the stairs, ran down to the first floor, and found Barnaby rummaging through the robbers' loot. He held up the remote, "Got it!" he said. "Sorry it took me so long to pick the lock."

"That's okay!" Babette said. "Beauregard was just in time."

✎ ✎ ✎ ✎ ✎

"Now we have a job for you, Oliver," Bridget said, when everyone had been introduced.

"Anything!" Oliver said. "Indeed, I think I owe you my life, and would be ever so happy to repay your kindness!"

They were out on the little lane around the corner from where Oliver had been imprisoned.

"If you turn the corner onto the main road up ahead, you'll come upon two men standing together," Bridget told the young boy.

"Yes?" he said.

"We need one of their wallets," Bridget said. "Either one will do."

Oliver looked troubled. "I had vowed that I'd never use the skills taught me by those evil robbers," he said. Then he smiled. "But as you are good people, I will do this for you."

The boy scurried down the street. When he was nearly at the corner, he stopped, turned, and smiled at his new friends. He then **commenced** on his mission.

In a moment, he appeared again behind the young travelers, for upon snatching the wallet, he had walked all the way around the block, and was out of sight before his victims knew he was gone.

"Oi!" Oliver called. The travelers turned and saw him holding up a wallet. "Easy as pie!"

"Good work, Oliver!" Barnaby said. He took the wallet and put it in the pocket of his lab coat.

"Now we'll escort you back to Mr. Brownlow's house," Bridget said.

The house in question was many blocks away, in a neighborhood known as Pentonville. While the group walked along, Oliver chattered happily about the kindness shown him there on his last visit, and worried aloud about whether he would be welcomed back.

"Mr. Brownlow may think I stole five pounds from him," Oliver said, his eyes downcast. "When last he saw me, he sent me on an errand to pay the book vendor. But Fagin took the banknote from me when he kidnapped me back, and now I'm returning with nothing."

"Mr. Brownlow will understand," Bridget assured the boy. "Once you explain what happened, everything will be fine."

"Stop! Police!" a gruff voice called from behind them.

"Uh oh," Bridget said.

The kids turned and saw two policemen bearing down, followed by the two men with glasses who had been shadowing the young travelers.

"Up against the wall!" the first policeman said. "Everyone!"

Bridget, Barnaby, Babette, and Oliver all put their hands up against the brick wall the cop was pounding on with his night stick.

"These gents say you kids stole one of their wallets," the policeman said. His partner searched the kids, beginning with Oliver. "If you've got it we're goin' ta find it!"

The second policeman searched Babette and Bridget, and then came to Barnaby, who appeared to be scratching his head.

"'Ands against the wall, I said!" the first policeman shouted. Barnaby slapped his hand against the wall.

"'Ere! Wot's this then?" the second policeman said. He pulled the brass remote from Barnaby's pocket.

"Well?" said the first. "Answer 'im, you young weasel! You got a species of **blunderbuss** on yer?"

"No, Sir!" Barnaby said.

"Well, what is it then?"

"It's an ionic fibrillator," Barnaby said, his voice shaking.

"A bionic whatzit?" the cop repeated. "'Ow does it work?"

"Allow me to demonstrate," Barnaby said. He turned around and flipped the switch on the brass wand.

The remote fizzed and crackled, wriggling slightly in the cop's hand. Then, a thin, crooked, blue beam shot out of the end of the wand, shooting straight up, turning the dull patch of gray London sky above them black. The policemen looked up just as a crash of thunder and a bolt of lightning joined a massive downpour. The shock of the thunder and lightning drove the policemen to their knees, gasping for breath in the **torrent**. Fence's henchmen were nowhere in sight.

"Let's go!" Bridget yelled. Barnaby lunged for the remote, which the cop had dropped, and scooped it up. Babette grabbed the astounded Oliver by the hand and dragged him along as the friends ran off down the street.

When they turned the corner, they had come out of the storm. Bridget stopped and took Oliver by the shoulders.

"Oliver," she said. "We've got to get to Big Ben. Can you get to Pentonville by yourself?"

"Yes!" the boy answered. "And thank you!"

"Thank you too, Oliver! Now run, and don't stop for anything!"

"I won't," Oliver Twist promised. Then he turned and scurried down the street.

Bridget, Babette, Barnaby, and Beauregard crossed London Bridge and fought their way across the boulevard full of carriages and pedestrians toward Big Ben. One after another, horses **reared** when Beauregard ran under their hooves. When the kids had nearly made it to the other side, Barnaby, who was the tallest of the group, saw Fence's henchmen working *their* way toward the clock tower too.

"Bridget! Look!" Barnaby shouted, pointing the two men out. But Bridget had already spotted them and, reaching open ground, was running as hard as she could toward the tower.

Beauregard, of course, was the one to reach it first. The door leading to the steep staircase was slightly ajar, and the big cat squeezed through it at a gallop. The kids were right behind him, and hit the stairs before their **bespectacled** pursuers reached the door. It was a hard climb, though, and Fence's henchmen began to gain on them.

"Come on, Barnaby!" Bridget shouted over her shoulder when she had almost reached the top. The young scientist was two flights below, with the two men nearly upon him. Bridget reached down over the railing to the next landing. "Grab my hand!"

Barnaby lunged and caught Bridget's hand and she hoisted him up the rest of the way to the top landing. The two scrambled into the tower chamber to find Babette looking out the window.

"Where's the exit to the continuum?" Bridget demanded.

"I don't know!" Babette said. "But Beauregard just jumped straight out the window!"

"Did he sort of disappear?" Barnaby asked, "Or did he keep falling?"

Bridget leaned out the window and looked down. She wasn't looking into inky blackness, but over London, gray and crowded, just as they'd left it.

"I don't know," Babette said. "I can't see him!"

"We'll have to risk it," Bridget said. She climbed up on the windowsill, and her two friends did the same. They were crouching there, arms around one another, when Fence's Henchmen burst into the tower from the stairs.

"One, two, three!" Bridget shouted. And the three friends tumbled out into the sky.

In the early chapters of Dickens's *Oliver Twist*, Oliver is sent to work for an undertaker. Read the passage below and then try to answer the questions that follow it.

> Oliver, being left to himself in the undertaker's shop, set the lamp down on a workman's bench, and gazed timidly about him with a feeling of awe and dread, which many people a good deal older than he, will be at no loss to understand. An unfinished coffin on black trestles, which stood in the middle of the shop, looked so gloomy and death-like that a cold tremble came over him, every time his eyes wandered in the direction of the dismal object: from which he almost expected to see some frightful form slowly rear its head, to drive him mad with terror. Against the wall were ranged, in regular array, a long row of elm boards cut into the same shape: looking in the dim light like high-shouldered ghosts with their hands in their breeches pockets. Coffin-plates, elm-chips, bright-headed nails, and shreds of black cloth, lay scattered on the floor; and the wall behind the counter was ornamented with a lively representation of two mutes in very stiff neckcloths, on duty at a large private door, with a hearse drawn by four black steeds, approaching in the distance. The recess behind the counter in which his flock mattress was thrust looked like a grave.

✍ DRILL #6 ✍

Answer the questions below.

1. Where is Oliver, in the passage above?
   a. in a jail cell
   b. in an undertaker's shop
   c. in a den of thieves

2. What kind of tree does Oliver's boss use for the construction of the coffins?
   a. pine
   b. beech
   c. elm

3. What's on the wall behind the counter?
   a. a picture of a hearse
   b. a dartboard
   c. a calendar with funeral plans marked

4. What's in the middle of the shop?
   a. a mean dog
   b. an accordion
   c. an empty coffin

5. It is safe to assume that Oliver is
   a. eager to assume his duties
   b. depressed and unhappy
   c. amiable and stoic

The answers can be found on page 171.

Chapter Six Glossary

adversary (ad' vər-ser' ē) (n.) a person who opposes or fights against another; opponent; enemy

aerodynamic (er' ō-di-nam' ik) (adj.) able to move efficiently, quickly, with little resistance, through the air

avail (ə-vāl') (n.) effective use or help

bespectacled (be-spek' tə-kəld) (adj.) wearing eyeglasses, spectacled

blunderbuss (blun' dər-bus') (n.) an obsolete, short gun with a large bore and a broad, flaring muzzle, accurate only at close range

brutish (broot' ish) (adj.) of or like a brute; savage, gross, stupid, irrational, etc.

chafe (chāf) (v.) irritate or make sore by rubbing; irritate or annoy in general

commence (kə-mens') (v.) begin; start

contemplate (kän' təm-plāt') (v.) to think about

dash (dash) (v.) to break by striking or knocking

feat (fēt) (n.) a notable deed

felon (fel' ən) (n.) a person guilty of a major crime; criminal

gizzard (giz' ərd) (n.) second stomach of a bird; (humorously) the stomach

jostle (jos' əl) (v.) to bump or push, as in a crowd

middling (mid' ling) (adj.) of middle size or quality; medium, ordinary

nocturnal (näk' tərn' əl) (adj.) functioning or active during the night

nonchalant (nän′ shə-länt′) (adj.) showing cool lack of concern; casually indifferent

peals (pēlz) (n.) the loud ringing of bells

physique (fi-zēk′) (n.) the structure, constitution, strength, form, or appearance of the body

protrude (prō-trōōd′) (v.) to stick out or thrust forward

rations (rash-ənz′) (n.) food

rear (rēr) (v.) to raise upright

regimen (rej′ ə-mən) (n.) a regulated system of diet, exercise, etc. for therapy or the maintenance or improvement of health

stealthily (stel′ thə-lē) (adv.) secretly, furtively, or slyly

streamlined (strēm-līnd′) (adj.) with no excess, as of fat, decoration, etc.; trim, simplified

syndicate (sin′ də-kit) (n.) an association of individuals or corporations formed to carry out some financial project; any group organized to further some undertaking; specifically, an association of criminals set up to control vice, gambling, etc.

teem (tēm) (v.) to become filled, overflowing

torrent (tor′ ənt) (n.) a swift, violent stream, especially of water; a very heavy rainfall

unsavory (un-sā′ vər ē) (adj.) unpleasant to taste or smell; offensive, disagreeable, or unpleasant; immoral

vices (vīs-əz) (n.) a defect, shortcoming

wonderment (wun′ dər-mənt) (n.) a state or expression of wonder; amazement; something causing wonder

Chapter 7
The Twenties Roar

I shan't, to avoid the indignity of overexcitement, go too deeply into what it was like to freefall over London in daylight. I had presumed that the west window of the clock tower was the passage back to the Continuum, since the wall of Professor Thorvaldson's office, through which we entered the dread passage, had been facing east. It was a rash decision, to be sure, but a rash decision was in order. I know you'll agree. For a long moment, I was under the impression that it was the *wrong* decision, as well. That is, I was definitely falling, but the pitch darkness that I had come to associate with the Continuum was not in evidence. When I leapt out the window, I expected to immediately be falling through that darkness. Instead, I found myself plummeting toward the ground beneath the clock tower, just as though I had . . . well, as though I'd leapt out a window. Falling, I looked down and saw the upturned faces of several Londoners, a proper gentleman in a silk top hat, a young girl—even the faces of several of the horses pulling carriages showed astonished expressions. Many people shielded their heads with their arms, no doubt afraid that I and my companions were headed straight for them. Their **evasive maneuvers**, at least, afforded me a chuckle. "No use covering up!" I thought. "If I land on you from the top of Big Ben, you're done for!"

But what of me, you ask? Wasn't I certain that I, too, was done for? I must confess that the thought crossed my mind as I hurtled toward the earth. It was coming up quickly and I could see the alarm in the blue eyes of the top-hatted gentleman.

Finally, what I had hoped and thought would happen did. The gray crowd of the great gathering of English humanity down there began to fade, as though a shadow were being cast by some giant. The image faded and faded until it became the black darkness of the Continuum. "Ah!" I thought to myself. "That was a bit of a jolt! Now just a tumble through the darkness and a somewhat abrupt stop—no problem. Who knows? Maybe it will be New York, once and for all!" As it happened, I wasn't far wrong. But it wasn't the New York we knew.

Bridget lifted her head, spat out a mouthful of sand, and coughed. She was still gathering her senses when she heard giggles.

"What on Earth is so funny!" she bellowed. The giggling stopped.

"Um—nothing," she heard Barnaby say.

"It is just that your face is covered with sand." Babette's voice was apologetic.

"Where are we now? Bridget asked, brushing the sand from her cheeks and nose and eyelids.

"Not a clue," Barnaby said. "So what else is new?"

"It is *trés beau*," Babette said. "Lovely."

Barnaby agreed. "I'll give you that."

Her eyes now reasonably clear of sand, Bridget pushed herself up on her knees and looked around. They were on a wide beach that stretched, in each direction, as far as the eye could see. Near where they had fallen, the tide came in, the waves rolling lazily up on the beach. A flock of seagulls wheeled overhead. Beauregard watched them intently.

"It *is* nice," Bridget said, "and familiar, somehow, too. But where is everybody?" The beach was deserted.

"Maybe they have gone home for the day," Babette guessed. "It is getting late." Indeed, the sun was low in the sky, the tide was low, and the breeze that the seagulls were hovering on was fairly cool.

Bridget stood up and brushed the sand off her clothes as best she could, stretching her sore muscles and wincing. "I hope it's not a desert island," she said.

"Improbable, fortunately," Barnaby said. "Those dunes look like North American shore formations. And there's no tropical plant life."

"And," Babette added, pointing down the beach, "there are houses over there."

"Houses!" her friends exclaimed, wheeling to look.

About a mile away the kids saw them: a cluster of white, clapboard houses dotting the dunes along the beach.

"Is anybody as hungry as I am?" Bridget asked. Even Beauregard, who was digging a very deep hole in the sand, started at the question, for none of them had eaten since the Marches had served them dinner in Massachusetts.

They started walking. Babette kicked off her black slippers and walked down to the water's edge, where the sand was hard-packed and the little waves rolled in over her bare feet. None of the kids spoke much; each of them was burdened by the **distinct** possibility that they'd never find their way back to the real world. Would they be trapped in a continual journey from one strange world to another, never at ease, or at home, ever again? Beauregard, for his part, kept the pace a dozen yards behind the kids, **harboring** some personal ideas about his next meal. He was tracking a large white gull as it dipped and soared above him.

The sun was sinking behind the dunes when the kids reached the first house. They walked up the wooden staircase and along the narrow walkway that led to the back door.

"Okay, guys," Bridget said. "Let me do the talking."

They stopped at the door and Bridget rapped on it. After a moment, she tried again, but no one answered.

"Hmm," Bridget mused. "I wonder where they went." She walked around the deck and turned the corner of the house, Babette and Barnaby in tow. They came to a large, sliding glass door, through which they could see into a living room cluttered with wicker furniture.

"Nice place," Bridget said.

"With a nice view," Babette said, looking out over the dunes to the water.

"Well," Barnaby said. "Nobody seems to be in."

"So what should we do?" Bridget looked at her two friends.

"It isn't bad to steal food if you're hungry," Babette said. "Is it?"

"I'd hate to be caught breaking in," Barnaby said.

"Let's try the next house," Bridget suggested.

The kids and cat walked around to the front of the deck, which looked out over a narrow, paved road. They climbed down the front staircase and walked down the road to the next house. It was the same story there. An empty garage and no answer at the door. They hit the road and kept going. It was almost completely dark now. The road had no electric lights on it, and the crickets were starting to chirp in the weeds alongside. The kids slapped their arms and necks to ward off mosquitoes.

After a while, they came to a stretch of road with no houses on it.

"Man," Bridget said. "It'd be nice to hit a town some time soon."

Just then, all four of them jumped at the sound of car horn. The car swept past them and kept going, its red tail lights winking at them as it continued on.

"Thanks a lot!" Bridget yelled after the car. "We don't mind walking!"

The kids stopped and caught their breath, watching the car recede into the night. The taillights came on again and then the car turned off the road.

"Hey, he's turning in someplace!" Barnaby exclaimed.

"Maybe it's a cafe," Babette said hopefully.

They started running along the road, keeping their sights on the spot where the car had disappeared. The moon was almost full, and they could see well enough to run. Soon they came upon an almost hidden turnoff, which they took. They hadn't gone very far along the path when they came across a whole row of parked cars. The cars looked like **antiques**: very few of them had roofs; all of them had big headlights that rested precariously on their big, round fenders. Bridget ran her hand over one of the cars' cute little doors.

"Listen," Babette said.

"What!" Barnaby whispered, alarmed.

"Shhh," Babette admonished. "Music."

They all listened and soon they heard the strains of a **gay** jazz tune played by what sounded like a live orchestra.

"That's strange music," Bridget noted. "It's like something my grandfather would play."

They listened some more.

"Well," Bridget said. "Maybe we should crash the party. What do you think?"

"I'm too hungry to think," Barnaby replied. "Let's just go."

It was, indeed, a party, the largest party on the largest lawn of the largest house any of them (except, perhaps, Beauregard) had ever seen. The lawn was dotted with tables with umbrellas that were draped with strings of colored lights. Here and there about the lawn groups of people talked and laughed **raucously**. Some danced, others sat at the tables, where they were waited on by uniformed caterers serving food and drinks. The orchestra was full sized, and was sitting at a free standing bandstand off to the side of the huge lawn. The house that presided over it all was a three-story mansion with a wide front staircase and massive columns. The kids stared at it all in awe from the cover of the line of trees that bordered the estate.

"I don't know about this," Bridget said.

"Why's everybody so dressed up?" Barnaby asked. It was true: The men all wore white or light-colored suits; the women wore gowns.

"It must be the twenties," Babette guessed. "The autos look like twenties autos, too."

"Well," Barnaby said. "At least we're in a book in our own century for once. That's something."

"But which book?" Bridget asked, looking down sharply when she felt Beauregard move against her legs. He was tracking a small animal in the underbrush.

"I don't even care!" said Barnaby bravely. "I need some of the food they're serving."

"Maybe we can slip up to one of the tables without anyone noticing," Bridget said. "Are you two ready?" Her friends nodded. They edged onto the lawn, Bridget in the lead.

Breezily, trying to seem unconcerned, the three friends walked across the wide, manicured lawn, dodging dancers, couples arm in arm, and waiters wearing tuxedos carrying full trays. They were forced to stop briefly when they were cut off by two young ladies, twins in matching yellow gowns, running toward a friend, a man with his arms open wide.

"Owen!" one of the girls squealed, "you've been simply **scandalous**!" The music swelled. Barnaby stared after the twins in astonishment. Bridget yanked on his arm.

"Don't stare!" she told him.

"But, they're . . ." he began.

"We're trying to look like we belong," she reminded him.

"Belong?" Barnaby said. "Everyone here is twice our age."

"Let's just get to a table!'

Finally they reached the other edge of the lawn and found a table with some space at it. Three people were seated there eating from plates heaped with finger foods and talking in loud, festive voices. The kids stood off to the side for a moment, then seated themselves gingerly in the empty seats. The people who were there, two men in snow-white suits and a young woman with short hair, scarcely seemed to notice their arrival.

"So has anyone met our host?" the girl asked.

"Not me," one of the men said. "But I know a fellow who knew him quite well at Oxford."

Bridget reached forward **surreptitiously** and grabbed one of the finger foods, examining it closely by the faint glow of the lights.

"Are you certain he went to Oxford?" the other man at the table asked.

"Well that's what he *says*, anyway," the woman answered with a big, knowing smirk.

"What is this?" Bridget whispered to Babette, who sat beside her, sunglasses on even in the dark. Babette knew a great deal about gourmet foods. The French girl leaned forward.

"It is a *canapé*," she told her friend.

"What's in it?" Bridget inquired.

"I'm sure it's fine," Barnaby said. He grabbed one of the *canapés* and bit into it **ravenously**. "It's good," he said, his mouth full.

"It is *fromage et . . .*" Babette began. "Uh . . . cheese on toast, or sometimes other things on toast," she corrected herself.

"I tell you I know a man who knew him there," the first man said. The party guests were still discussing their host and his college career.

"Well that's not what I heard," the woman said, as a waiter appeared with a tray of glasses. Each of the guests took one. The waiter held the tray down so that the kids could each take one. They did. The glasses were filled to the brim with bubbly liquid. Barnaby held his up to his nose and sniffed.

"It's champagne!" he said.

"I guess the waiter didn't realize we're kids," Bridget said. "Have you ever had it?"

"Nope," Barnaby said. "Have you?"

Bridget shook her head. But Babette said, "I have, a few times. In France, parents let their kids have a little wine with dinner sometimes."

"Champagne is wine?" Bridget asked.

"Yes," Babette said. "It is a *kind* of wine."

Bridget sniffed her glass and tasted the champagne. "Ick!" She made a face and pushed her glass away, grabbing another *canapé* with her other hand. "You like this stuff?"

Babette shrugged. "It's okay."

"Pray tell, darling," the first man at the table said to the sarcastic woman next to him. "What have you heard about our dear host that we haven't? Some delightfully **prurient** rumor, I suppose." Now *he* was being sarcastic.

"Yes," the other man chimed in. "Tell. I'm jealously uninformed."

"Well!" the woman said. "I heard that Mr. Gatsby didn't inherit his money at all, that he came to be wealthy some other way."

"What way?" the second man asked.

"Yes, what way?" said the other. "Moving pictures? Counter-feiting?"

"Let us just say that **Prohibition** has been very kind to him!" the woman said, laughing. She dropped her voice to a hushed, deep tone. "And they even say he once killed a man!"

"Preposterous!" the first man said, dropping his sarcasm in favor of an indignant snort. "My source is **eminently** more reliable than yours. Gatsby went to Oxford and fought in the war. His family is immensely rich in oil fields, or orange groves, or something."

"Indeed!" the woman said giggling. "You'd think the two of you had been in diapers together."

"I'm getting another drink," the man said curtly. He stood up, straightening his tie.

"Oh! Get me one, too!" the woman squealed. "On second thought, dance with me, you sensitive boy. Or we'll get a drink and then dance!" She hurried after him. The second man followed.

"But that's not what I heard at all," he called after them.

Bridget swallowed the last of her second *canapé* and waited until the three party guests were out of earshot. "Guys," she said. "I think I know what book we're in."

"Yo' dough?" Barnaby said. His mouth was still full of food. For a skinny guy, he sure could eat a lot.

"Didn't you hear what those people were saying?" Bridget asked. "Prohibition? Gatsby?"

Barnaby perked up, still chewing. *"Na Geet Gassmee!"* he mumbled excitedly.

"The Great Gatsby?" Babette inquired more coherently.

"By F. Scott Fitzgerald," Bridget confirmed. "Have you read it?" Babette shook her head.

"I have," Barnaby said after swallowing. "Boy! That means we're on Long Island. And that's Long Island Sound." He turned to his right and pointed across the immense lawn, toward the dark, calm water. "We're less than a hundred miles from New York City!"

"Yeah," Bridget said, frowning. "But New York in the *nineteen-twenties*. Don't get too carried away."

Barnaby was instantly deflated. But then he brightened again. "Maybe the continuum moves closer to our world in certain places. We're in the twentieth century; we're in New York. Maybe we're getting closer."

Bridget shook her head. "I'm not convinced. We're still in a book, not the real world. Until we figure out how to get back there, we're still lost."

"Well," Barnaby said, "while we've been running around, I've been thinking about this problem. Why are Fence's henchmen able to follow us from book to book at will, but we have no idea where we'll end up next? It seems like they know more about the continuum than we do, like how to steer through it."

"But why didn't Professor Thorvaldson tell us how to steer, if there's a way?" Bridget asked.

"Maybe he doesn't know about it," Barnaby said. "Maybe when Fence co-opted the continuum he had some **metaphysicians** in his stable of experts examine it, and maybe they discovered properties that even Thorvaldson didn't know about."

"Hmm," Bridget said, her brow furrowed. The orchestra had started a slow number, and a few couples who had been vigorously **fox-trotting** paused to catch their breath and take up the waltz. "So, if we can interrogate Fence's henchmen, maybe they'll tell us how they pick and choose which books to enter."

"But how will we get them to tell us?" Babette wondered. "It is hard for three kids to intimidate two adults."

"That's true," Bridget admitted. "We'll have to think. But let's go somewhere more private. I'm starting to feel a little too **conspicuous** now that the party's dying down."

The kids got up and edged away from the festivities, down toward the edge of the lawn, where a thin band of shore separated the grass from the water of the sound. They walked in single file along the little beach until Gatsby's property was hidden from view behind them. It was a clear summer night, and the stars were out.

Soon, the kids came upon a little pier, where a powerboat was moored. At the end of the dock, a man stood very straight with his hands in his pockets. He was fair haired and sturdy, dressed in a pale, pink suit. Bridget stopped before stepping onto the dock and held her arm out to restrain her friends.

"Wait!" she whispered. "Look."

"It's Gatsby," Barnaby said.

The man didn't turn around, or seem to hear anything, just stared **intently** at something across the water.

"Certainly?" Babette asked.

"Yeah," Barnaby said, still watching the man. "He's looking across the sound at the green light on Daisy Buchanan's dock."

"Daisy Buchanan?" Babette said inquiringly.

"She's the woman Gatsby's in love with," Barnaby told her. "But she's married to someone else."

The man stirred, as though alerted to the fact that he wasn't alone. The kids started momentarily, but Gatsby didn't turn around, just changed his position slightly, in the way someone does who has been standing still for a very long time. He kept gazing across the water.

"Do you think he can help us figure out a way to stop Fence?" Bridget asked.

"Well," Barnaby looked up at the stars, thinking. "He does have some henchmen of his own. Maybe he'll lend us some."

"We don't want anybody to get hurt," Bridget said. "Do we?"

"I don't," Babette replied.

"No," Barnaby said. "I guess that's out." The kids were stumped again.

They were so lost in **rumination** that they didn't hear Gatsby turn and walk toward them along the wooden boards of the dock. Gatsby, in turn, was too absorbed in his thoughts to notice their little group, and consequently he walked right into Barnaby, who jumped a foot.

"Excuse me, old sport," Gatsby said, smiling charmingly. His pink suit seemed to glow in the warm night. "I didn't see you there. I'm certain we've met before."

"Um . . . I don't think so," Barnaby said, inadvertently shying away from the fictional millionaire.

"Jay Gatsby," the man said, and bowed to each of them.

"I'm Bridget," Bridget told him, "and these are my friends Babette and Barnaby. We've just been at your party."

Gatsby nodded distractedly and looked up toward his estate as though listening to the faint strains of the orchestra. Then he turned back to Bridget and smiled again.

"Enjoying yourselves, I trust," he said. "Up from town, eh?"

"Yes," Bridget answered. "And we're having a heck of a time getting back."

Gatsby seemed not entirely to be listening. He was fidgeting and looking at the ground.

"Really?" he said. "Will you walk with me? I've got to get back to the house. Expecting a call."

The group of them—the mysterious host and his **entourage** of kids—started strolling back along the beach.

"So you say you can't get home," Gatsby said.

"That's right," said Bridget.

"What's the trouble?" their host asked. "Flat tire? My man'll fix you right up. Or I'll send you with my chauffeur."

"Thanks very much, sir," Bridget said. "But we're going to need more help than that."

The group was traversing the lawn, passing the last dancers of the evening and the tired-looking musicians on the bandstand.

"Really?" Gatsby said, stopping at the foot of the stairs to his mansion. He looked out over the **dwindling** crowd of people on his vast lawn. "You'll have to tell me all about it, as soon as I've finished my calls." Gatsby tipped his head toward the large open doorway, which afforded a view into the front hall, blazing with light. "Come on in. You can wait for me in the library."

The kids timidly followed the host into his incredible house. In the gargantuan sitting room, a young woman sat at a grand piano, playing for a group of admirers who leaned against the instrument in a variety of slack poses. As the woman played, great, big tears rolled down her cheeks, creating long tracks of mascara on her face. Many armchairs were arrayed about the room, and most of them were occupied by people who were asleep.

"Right in there," Gatsby said to the kids without stopping as he passed the library door. "I won't be a moment." The kids pushed the door open and went inside.

What they beheld when they entered the library rivaled the one they'd been to in New York. Stacks of books lined every wall except one, from the floor to the forty-foot ceiling. A ladder on wheels was **affixed** to a brass track, which was fastened to the bookcases by screws and traveled the perimeter of the room. The kids looked around at the masses of cloth-bound volumes, **flabbergasted**.

"They're all real," a voice said from across the room. "I've inspected them."

Barnaby tore his gaze from the books on the walls and looked toward the voice. The others did the same.

"Owl-eyes!" Barnaby said, without meaning to.

"That's a bit rude," the man said. He wore spectacles with round wire frames and thick lenses that made the eyes behind them look huge, like an owl's. "Just because I'm blind and in need of contraptions. You've got 'em too, sir, if I'm not mistaken."

"I'm sorry," Barnaby said. "I just . . . I thought . . ."

"We thought you were someone else," Bridget interjected, "someone we knew."

"A common **affliction**," the man said. He was sitting on the edge of the long table that ran down the center of the library, kicking his legs back and forth. "I must say I'm worried about how I'll get back to town. I had a ride but I can't find the fellow who brought me. Are you going back tonight, by any chance?"

"Well," Bridget hemmed, looking at Babette, then back at the man, "we may be."

But the man hadn't waited for her reply. He let himself down from the table, seemed on the verge of kneeling, then righted himself. He looked up at the ceiling.

"Whoo! What drives a man to **accumulate** such **regal trappin's**?" he asked nobody in particular. "Where's the ambition to get and get, more and more, as it's so much mirage, especially for our strange host, I hear."

The kids looked at each other and then back at the man, who was straightening his glasses **meticulously** on his rather pink face.

"The absolute conviction that he'll wake up tomorrow back where he started is what," the man continued, answering his own question. "And he will wake up there, Gatsby will. There's not a question in my mind."

"Or maybe he's trying to impress someone," Barnaby said. "Someone who was unattainable when he was poor."

"Ah!" Owl-eyes said. "Is it a fresh bit of news you have then? Please share it! Who would Mr. Gatsby be trying to impress?"

Bridget hurriedly shook her head. "No! It was just a guess," she said. "We know as little about him as you do."

"Indeed?" Owl-eyes replied. He seemed confused, even transported somewhere else for a moment. Then he gathered himself and smiled.

"Well! It certainly was enlightening conversing with you," he said cheerfully. "Now I must find the driver of my **conveyance**. It's frightfully late, you see." The odd man slouched toward the door and made his way out into the living room. He left the door ajar, and the kids could hear the stumbling piano playing of the woman with the mascara.

"He's right," Bridget said. "It's late and I'm sort of tired. All this running around is hard work."

"Perhaps we can find an empty room and nap for a while," Babette suggested.

"Don't you think we should check this out first?" Barnaby reached into his mass of hair and pulled out Fence's henchman's wallet.

"I almost forgot!" Bridget was wide awake again at the sight of the wallet. "Picking that guy's pocket in London seems like years ago. Let's see what's in it!"

Barnaby took the wallet and opened it on the table; the others gathered around him. There were some credit cards and a driver's license, which pictured one of the men the kids had seen in London. His name was Paul V. Richardson.

"Nothing here helps us get home," Barnaby said.

"Wait," Bridget cautioned, taking the wallet. She opened it lengthwise, inspecting the space where the money was kept. Richardson had a few American dollars, some British pounds, and a slip of paper folded in thirds. "What's this?" Bridget asked, taking out the paper and unfolding it.

"It looks like a poem," Babette said.

Here is what the paper said:

> To alight in verse or tale,
>
> firm in mind its title keep
>
> To return from whence you hail,
>
> think just one word before you leap:
>
> *Home.*

"Yes!" Bridget shouted. "We're going back to New York, guys!"

"You mean all this time we could have gone home just by thinking about it?" Babette asked.

"It seems that way," Bridget replied, folding up the paper and shoving it in her jacket pocket. She reached into her other pocket and brought out a fresh piece of bubblegum, which she unwrapped and stuck into her mouth.

"That doesn't make sense," Barnaby asserted, considering it. "I've been thinking about that every time we entered the Continuum."

"Maybe your thoughts were a jumble," Bridget countered, "and certain things you, or I, or Babette were thinking were steering us astray. *"Think one word: Home,"* is what the paper says. Maybe if we do that, literally think the word, the Continuum will steer us straight back."

"It's worth a try," Barnaby said. "Let's get back to the beach."

Outside Gatsby's mansion, the party was breaking up. One of the guests, driving rather recklessly, had run his car into the stone wall lining the border of the estate, and broken his front axle in half. A crowd had gathered around the car and was trying to convince the driver that the car was totaled. He remained unconvinced, and kept pressing the accelerator, producing a loud grinding noise. Sitting nearby, regarding the commotion with an **impassive** air, was Beauregard, who had spent most of the party securing food for himself. When the kids slipped off Gatsby's property, they saw him there. Bridget called to him.

"Come on, Beauregard," she said. "We're finally going home."

Trudging back the way they had come along the dark road, the kids became bothered by a nagging suspicion that it would be rather difficult to find the hole in the sand that they were looking for.

"We can just find those first houses we tried to break into," Babette said. "And then walk a mile past them."

"It's a wide beach," Barnaby said **pessimistically**. "And it's dark! We'll have to be pretty lucky."

"Quiet, Barnaby!" Bridget said. "In times of great stress, **fatalism** is an unwelcome attitude, even if it's the only one that makes sense."

In a moment, the second **repository** of Barnaby's doubt was no more. The sun began to rise. Out along the horizon, a gleam appeared, and the darkness began to fade. Up ahead along the road, the kids could see the **silhouettes** of a group of houses.

"Wow!" Bridget said. "We were at that party all night long!"

"I'm not tired at all," Barnaby said.

"Me neither," Bridget replied.

"It is nice to see the sun coming up," Babette noted.

When they had passed the houses, the kids climbed over the dunes and onto the beach. It was pretty as ever: waves rolling in, gulls wheeling on a gentle breeze overhead. They walked down to the water's edge and continued along, keeping an eye on the center of the beach as they walked, so they wouldn't miss the entrance to the Continuum.

After awhile, Babette said, "Maybe we should move to the center, in case we should miss it."

"Good idea," Bridget said, and the four friends climbed the incline to the middle of the beach. They strolled along in the early morning sunshine. And strolled along. And strolled along. The sun rose higher and started to burn hotter. The long night of **revelry** at Gatsby's house was beginning to take its toll.

"Man!" Bridget exclaimed. "Where is that hole?"

Barnaby stopped walking. "Do you think we missed it?" he asked. He looked back at the houses on the dunes. "Those houses look a mile away at least."

"We couldn't have missed it!" Bridget said with conviction, though what she was basing her conviction on nobody knew. "Where could it be?"

Then she saw a spectacular sight. Off to the left of where Bridget was standing, Beauregard sat and watched a gull hovering above the sand. The cat waited and waited to make his move, but the gull didn't waver from its position, about ten feet in the air. Beauregard seemed to lose interest, turning and walking away. Then the big bird lowered itself to the sand, but before it could land it was suddenly sucked under, and disappeared.

"What the? . . ." Bridget said, startled. The others turned to look where she was looking.

Another seagull, perhaps looking for the first, flew over and came in for a landing on the sand. It too, comimg within two or three feet of its destination, it too was sucked violently downward and disappeared under the sand.

"Could it be the entrance to the Continuum?" Barnaby asked.

"I don't see what else it could be," Bridget answered. "Unless there's quicksand on Long Island."

"I don't remember any mention of quicksand in *The Great Gatsby*," Barnaby said.

"Then we are almost home," Babette said calmly. She held out her hands to her friends. "Are you ready?"

"Am I ever!" Bridget said. She took one of Babette's hands and Barnaby took the other. Beauregard sidled up beside the three kids. "Remember to think *home*!" Bridget reminded the others. "One, two, thr . . ."

"Hold on!" a voice shouted. It was a male voice, high-pitched and quavering. The kids stopped and looked around.

The two men they'd hired Oliver Twist to pickpocket in London were walking toward them across the sand. The one in the suit jacket and jeans was in the lead.

"I believe you have something of mine," he said.

"Oh yeah," Bridget said. "Barnaby, give the man his wallet."

Barnaby reached into his hair and brought out the wallet. He threw it to the man, who caught it awkwardly against his chest.

"Sorry about that," Bridget told the two men. "But we needed instructions on how to get home. Now, if you'll excuse us, we're late for supper."

"I'm afraid I can't do that," the man whose name was Richardson replied. He straightened his glasses. "You see, we know what your mission is, and it's our job to see that you don't get back to New York yet."

The kids looked at each other. Then back at the men who faced them across the dip in the sand that was the entrance to the Continuum. "Is Fence that afraid of us?" Bridget asked. "We're just a bunch of kids."

The man smiled. He put the wallet in his pocket. "Your **exploits** are well-known. And you're looking for a way to stop Mr. Fence from carrying out his print-to-screen project. We'd like to know what you've found."

"What if we don't tell you?" Bridget asked. "Excuse me for saying so, but you're not very **menacing**. Are you armed?"

The two men looked at each other and burst out laughing. Their honking laughs sent a nearby group of gulls flying out over the water.

The first man spoke up. "No, we don't carry any weapons. With a word from us, our boss can have your parents' credit ratings slashed, if necessary." The kids were startled by the threat. "But," Mr. Richardson continued, "Mr. Fence prefers a more **subtle** approach. For now, we can simply keep you trapped in the Land of Fiction for a very long time."

It was Bridget's turn to laugh. "But how? We read the poem. We can go home anytime we want to."

"I don't think so," Richardson said.

"Oh yeah?" Bridget challenged. "Watch. Join hands, guys." Babette and Barnaby did as she said. "And think *home*. On three. One, two, three!"

As they leapt, the bespectacled man named Richardson yelled one word that lodged in the brains of each of the four friends. It was the title of one of the greatest plays ever written in English or any other language, conceived by the greatest dramatic mind of all time.

The word was *Hamlet*.

Some English teachers will request that you take your own notes on the books that you are reading for class, and not just on the lectures. If they require you to do this, and ask to check the notes to monitor your progress, consider yourself lucky. It's a good thing to have some outside motivation to get into the habit of taking notes. Even if your notes are just a list of the book's characters, with a short description of each character and a summary of his or her role in the story, it's a good way of keeping track of what the author is trying to say. This will especially help you when you are reading novels with multiple characters and locations and complicated themes.

The Great Gatsby is a fairly straightforward story with a moderate number of characters drawn in brief sketches. The book concerns the tragedy of living for a long time with an unrealistic dream, and what the consequences are to the dreamer when the dream is shattered. Read what F. Scott Fitzgerald writes about the mysterious, seductive Gatsby, and then try to answer the questions that follow.

> He smiled understandingly—much more than understandingly. It was one of those rare smiles with a quality of eternal reassurance in it, that you may come across four or five times in life. It faced— or seemed to face—the whole external world for an instant, and then concentrated on *you* with an irresistible prejudice in your favor. It understood you just as far as you wanted to be understood, believed in you as you would like to believe in yourself, and assured you that it had precisely the impression of you that, at your best, you hoped to **convey**. Precisely at that point it vanished—and I was looking at an elegant, young roughneck, a year or two over thirty, whose elaborate formality of speech just missed being absurd. Some time before he introduced himself, I'd got a strong impression that he was picking his words with care.

Answer the questions that follow.

1. What makes Gatsby so appealing to others?

   a. his wealth

   b. his elegance

   c. his smile

2. What quality in Gatsby's smile does the narrator emphasize?

   a. its understanding

   b. its sarcasm

   c. its emptiness

3. What conclusion does the narrator seem to draw about Gatsby's origins?

   a. Gatsby was born in the upper classes

   b. Gatsby was born poor and became rich recently

   c. Gatsby was a lieutenant in the First World War

4. How does the narrator draw this conclusion?

   a. by noting Gatsby's necktie, which is inappropriate

   b. by noting Gatsby's carefully formal speech

   c. by noting Gatsby's war medals

5. What does the term "roughneck" probably mean?

   a. cowboy

   b. chauffeur

   c. rough, coarse person

The answers can be found on page 171.

Chapter Seven Glossary

accumulate (ə-kyōōm' yə-lāt') (v.) amass, collect, or gather

affix (ə-fiks') (v.) fasten, join, or attach (usually used with "to")

affliction (ə-flik' shən) (n.) a state of pain, distress, or grief

antique (an-tēk') (n.) of or belonging to the past; not modern

conspicuous (kən-spik' yōō-əs) (adj.) easily seen or noticed; readily observable

convey (kən-vā') (v.) to carry, bring, or take from one place to another; to impart (information)

conveyance (kən-vā' əns) (n.) a means of transportation, especially a vehicle

distinct (di-stingkt') (adj.) clear to the senses or intellect, plain, definite, unmistakable

dwindle (dwin' dl) (v.) become smaller and smaller, shrink, waste away

eminent (em' ə-nənt) (adj.) high in station, rank or repute; distinguished

entourage (än' too-räzh) (n.) a group of personal attendants

evasive (ē-va' sîv) (adj.) tending or seeking to evade; elusive

exploit (ek' sploit') (n.) a striking or notable deed; feat

fatalism (fat' l-iz' əm) (n.) the acceptance of or submission to fate

flabbergast (flab′ ər-gast′) ((adj.) (informal) amazed, astonished, astounded

fox-trot (fäks′ trät′) (n.) a social dance, performed by couples, characterized by various combinations of short, quick steps

gay (gā) (adj.) joyous, cheerful, light-hearted

harbor (här′ bər) (n.) to keep or hold in the mind; maintain; entertain

impassive (im-pas′ iv) (adj) without emotion, apathetic, unmoved

intently (in-tent′ lē) (adv.) with great concentration and determination

maneuver (mə-nōō′ vər) (n.) an adroit move, skillful proceeding, etc., especially as characterized by craftiness

metaphysician (met′ ə-fi-zish′ ən) (n.) a person who creates or develops metaphysical (highly abstract) theories

meticulous (mə-tik′ yōō-ləs) (adj.) extremely careful about small details

pessimistic (pəs′ əmis′ tik) (adj.) pertaining to or characterized by pessimism; gloomy

Prohibition (pro′ ə-bish′ ən) (n.) the period from 1920 to 1933, when the sale of alcoholic beverages in the U.S. was forbidden by an amendment to the Constitution

prurient (prōōr′ ē-ənt) (adj.) having or tending to have lascivious or lustful thoughts

quaver (kwā′ vər) (v.) to shake tremulously, quiver or tremble

raucous (rô′ kəs) (adj.) harsh, strident, grating

ravenous (rav′ ə-nəs) (adj.) extremely hungry, famished

regal (rē′gəl) (adj.) of or pertaining to a king, royal

repository (ri-päz′ ə-tor′ ē) (n.) a receptacle or place where things are stored

revelry (rev′ əl-rē) (n.) reveling, boisterous festivity

rumination (rōō′ mə-nā shən) (noun) meditation, musing, or pondering

scandalous (skan′ dəl-əs) (adj.) disgraceful, shameful, or shocking; improper

silhouette (sil′ ōō-et′) (n.) a dark image outlined against a lighter background

subtle (sut′ l) (adj.) fine or delicate in meaning or intent; difficult to perceive or understand

surreptitious (sər′ əp-tish′ əs) (adj.) acting in a stealthy way

trappings (trap′ ings) (n.) articles of equipment or dress, especially of an ornamental character

Chapter 8
To Be or Not to Be

Well, at least we knew where we were going this time. I was even a bit curious to visit Elsinore, the royal castle of Denmark, as it is so beautiful and mysterious in William Shakespeare's wonderful play. During one of my **stints** as a housecat back home, I lived with an old Southern family in a sprawling, rickety house outside Charleston—I believe their name was Quimby. Anyway, the matriarch of the family was an ancient lady who **doted** on me and wore a **pince-nez**. A lovely woman! She never failed to give me the scraps from her dinner, of which there were plenty, as she was a very light eater. She did this over the protests of her son, who still lived at home though he was past thirty in human years. Junior kept repeating the fact that the family fortune wasn't nearly as large as it had once been and they couldn't afford to "waste" perfectly good food on an "animal," and blah, blah, blah. Why, if money was so tight, he wasn't out securing himself **gainful** employment instead of trying to undermine my relationship with his dear mother is a mystery to me. As it happened, this odious mama's boy finally succeeded in turning my benefactor against me, and I was forced to **vacate** the premises. But that is a story for another time.

While I was still in her good graces, Mrs. Quimby made it a practice of presiding over nightly readings in the grand sitting room of her lovely home. Her son would naturally be in attendance, as would any number of callers. The old lady was a much-beloved and admired presence in her community and drew a steady stream of **illustrious** visitors. Curled up at her feet I heard the matchless poetry of Shakespeare for the first time, the tragedies, the histories, the comedies, and the sonnets. Those were lively and educational evenings! First, Mrs. Quimby would read, in her gently trembling, tasteful voice. Invariably, though, her son would take it upon himself to wrest the reading duties from her, admonishing his mother not to strain her vocal chords. At such times, I found it necessary to leave the room, as I could hardly bear the man's brutish rendering of the Bard's delicate words. (I daresay several of Mrs. Quimby's guests chose that very moment to take their leave as well!) Proceeding to the back door, I would slip outside and seek the adventures of the night.

But now I was falling again. My young companions weren't yelling as they once had while hurtling through the Continuum. After all they'd been through, they were **steeled** to whatever awaited them on the other side. I was proud of them. Then, suddenly, I was under them! Flat on my stomach, I slithered out from the pile, sat up, and set to grooming. When that was finished, I could take stock of my surroundings. But not before.

✎ ✎ ✎ ✎ ✎

Babette came to on her back, with a little of the wind knocked out of her, her long legs dangling over Bridget, who was flat on her face again. Through her dark glasses, Babette could see Barnaby, ten feet above her, struggling in the branches of a black, leafless tree.

"Help me down!" Barnaby cried. The branches had caught in his lab coat and the cuff of one of the legs of his pants, so that he looked like a large, bushy-headed **marionette** suspended above a stage. "Help! Please!" he yelled again.

"Hold your horses, Barnaby," Bridget said softly. She sounded tired. "Let us catch our breath." Babette took her legs off Bridget's back and both girls got to their feet. They looked up at Barnaby, who had stopped struggling and was just hanging there. The tree trunk was bare of branches below six or seven feet, so there was no way for either of the girls to climb up.

"Perhaps if you stand on my shoulders," Babette suggested, lacing the fingers of her hands together to form a foothold for Bridget's sneaker. Bridget considered this.

"I don't know," she said finally. "Are you sure you can lift me?"

Babette shrugged. "I *think* I can," she said.

"While you two are discussing the matter, maybe that lazy cat can get me down!" Barnaby said heatedly. The girls turned to Beauregard, who had not yet finished grooming his fur.

"I didn't think of that!" Bridget exclaimed. "Beauregard!"

The cat looked up for a moment, then turned and looked into the distance, as though something of much greater importance were taking place there.

"Come on, Beauregard," Bridget **cajoled** him. "Help Barnaby down."

After a moment's more hesitation, Beauregard turned and walked up to the tree. He sat back on his **haunches** and regarded the suspended Barnaby, who wriggled pathetically for effect.

"Please?" the scientist said.

At that, Beauregard scurried up the tree trunk like a squirrel, digging his claws into the bark and appearing almost instantly on the branch that had a hold of Barnaby's lab coat's right shoulder. He calmly walked to the end of the branch and nudged the lab coat off the tip with his nose.

Barnaby gave a yelp as he flipped over, fell a few feet, hit a lower branch, and toppled to the ground at the girls' feet.

"Are you okay?" Babette asked.

"Naturally," Barnaby said, as Beauregard plopped gracefully down beside him. "I love falling out of trees onto my head."

"Here's your stuff," Bridget said, handing Barnaby the fibrillator remote, as well as a few other odds and ends that had fallen out of his hair.

"Thank you," Barnaby said, standing up and taking his things, depositing some of them in the pockets of his lab coat and others back in his hair.

"Let's look around," Bridget said. "Maybe we can find the entrance back into the Continuum and get home before those men follow us here. I knew I shouldn't stand there talking to them! They just yell out 'Hamlet,' and suddenly we've all got the title in our heads, and here we are."

Babette looked around, peering into the thick fog. "I wonder which way the castle is."

"Oh, no!" Bridget said. "You want to meet Hamlet, don't you!"

Babette looked at the ground, ashamed. "He is my favorite character in English literature."

"But if we don't leave now, Fence's men will arrive and pull the same thing they did back in Long Island!" Bridget reasoned.

"I guess you're right," Babette admitted.

"Yeah," Barnaby said. "I'm with you Bridget. Let's find the Continuum and go home right now!"

"I shouldn't think, wherever your home may be, that you should find it missing when you doth make your return," a strong, deep voice said from high above them. The kids looked up slowly and saw a man **astride** a huge, beautiful horse. The man drew his sword and held it at his side. "But I must insist, now I find you **unbidden** in this wood, that you come along to Elsinore and face the judgment of my lord."

Bridget looked at Babette, who couldn't hide a tiny smile.

"Shut up," Bridget whispered, though Babette hadn't said a word.

Another man galloped up on horseback; stopping just short of the group, the horse reared, and the kids jumped back, scared half to death. If you've ever seen a horse rear in real life, you'll know how they felt.

"What, ho, Marcellus! Some uncommon **quarry** have you captured here," the new arrival said.

"Indeed, they are," the first knight said.

"What are their origins?" asked the second. "Their **vestments** place them in some unknown tribe. How strangely they are attired!"

"Look who's talking," Bridget whispered to Babette, for both knights were dressed head to toe in close-fitting animal hides, draped here and there with iron plates and chain mail for protection. Bridget was annoyed at their gloating.

"Come Barnardo!" said the first knight, Marcellus. "Take on your horse the slender lad with tunic of snowy hue. I shall **fain** take the others."

It was Barnaby's turn to be annoyed, though he kept his voice down.

"What is it with characters in books?" he asked. "I wear a lab coat, not a tunic."

"What say ye, young sportsman?" said Marcellus in a booming voice. He would have been menacing, but Barnardo burst out laughing at the reference to Barnaby as a "sportsman." Marcellus reached out and grabbed the collar of Barnaby's lab coat, lifting the boy into the air and holding him motionless as easily as the tree had. He looked the frightened young scientist in the eye. "Mark it well. T'would **behoove** you hold your tongue 'til in my prince's chamber you do dwell." With little effort, the knight swung Barnaby onto the back of his horse. The other knight, Barnardo, taking each girl's arm in turn, hoisted Bridget and Babette onto the back of his own giant steed. The two knights then kicked their horses and set off with their prisoners to present them to Prince Hamlet. As they left the forest, Bridget looked back over her shoulder, wondering where Beauregard had gotten to now.

At first, the kids were not aware that they had left the wood, as the fog was so thick they could only see a few feet in front of the horses' noses. But presently they came upon an open clearing, and as a chilly breeze blew across the field, a shroud of fog lifted from the hill beyond. Then they caught their breath.

It was a real castle, all right, perched at the top of the low, broad hill. A hundred yards wide, a hundred feet tall, complete with **turrets** and **spires**, **battlements** and a single soaring archway, where a drawbridge was already lowering as they approached the wide moat.

The drawbridge hit the grassy bank of the moat with a solid thud, and the horses mounted it without breaking stride, their shod hooves clacking on the hard, sturdy beams. Bridget looked up at the archway as the horses passed under it and saw the spiked bottom of the black iron door suspended to let them pass. She glanced to the top of the castle walls, where there were **sentries** posted, standing motionless. All three kids were awestruck.

Inside the castle walls was a huge dirt-floored courtyard, crowded with people. Some were loading things onto carts. Others were apparently passing through on urgent business, purposefully hurrying through the crowd from one wing of the castle to another. Still others seemed not to be doing much of anything, killing time in small groups, fooling around with their swords, washing and feeding horses. The two knights rode on.

Reaching the very rear of the courtyard, where the gray wall lined with blue windows shot straight up eighty feet in the air, each knight dismounted and helped his prisoners to the ground. Opening a barely visible door, its wood the same color as the surrounding stone, Marcellus **bade** the kids follow him with a wave of his chain-gloved hand. Barnardo took up the rear.

They climbed. The staircase was steep, narrow, and dark. Reaching out to touch the stone wall, Barnaby found it slick with **condensation**. This was a cold and wet part of the world! Up and up they went, coming occasionally to small landings lit by the rooms they opened onto. When Babette tried to sneak a peek into the first great hall they came to, Barnardo put a stop to it.

"Eyes ahead!" he barked. She didn't peek again.

Five flights they climbed, six, seven. On the seventh landing, Marcellus halted abruptly and turned to the right, adopting a stiff, military bearing.

"Tarry here," he cautioned the three friends, "whilst I **importune** on thine account. Thou might elect to use these moments well, and pray his lordship should not choose to behead thee." At that, the knight proceeded into the chamber, leaving the kids standing in the damp and shadowy stairwell. Bridget dared not turn to look at her friends' faces. She was fairly certain that they were as frightened as she was.

Standing as still as possible in the shadows, the kids could hear the muffled but strong voice of Marcellus but couldn't make out the words. After he spoke, there was a silence, then a barely audible reply from some other man. Babette couldn't believe it. Was she about to be ushered into the presence of the Prince of Denmark?

After a few more unbearably long moments, her question was answered. Marcellus called out: "Barnardo! Bring your mysterious prisoners forth!"

"Move along!" Barnardo ordered. Bridget stumbled forward into the chamber, followed by Barnaby and Babette. Almost as soon as they entered, they were ordered to halt.

This was no great soaring hall, as they had expected it to be. Instead, the kids found a cramped and cluttered attic-type room, furnished with heavy, wooden chairs and a table. The walls were bare, and the panes of glass in the window were plain, unlike the fancy blue stained glass they had seen in the windows that overlooked the courtyard. The single adornment in the window was the hunched figure of a young man, plainly dressed in coarse cloth, sitting cross-legged in the window seat. The man did not look up when the kids filed in. He was staring into the face of a human skull set before him on the sill.

"On your knees, prisoners!" Marcellus said sternly. He tapped the back of Bridget's knee and she knelt and bent her head. Her friends did the same.

"Please rise," the man in the window said without looking up. His voice was faint and hoarse. The kids stood up, adjusting shakily to keep their balance as they did so. "What brings you to Elsinore?"

The young travelers found themselves unable to reply.

"You would do well to answer the prince's inquiry!" Marcellus told them.

"Patience, my friend," Hamlet said softly, for it was Hamlet. "**Mayhap** their tale, be it fact or fiction, requires some care in the telling. We may extend them the courtesy of a moment in which they may collect themselves. At your leisure, guests, come ye to Elsinore as friend or foe?" The prince turned finally and regarded the kids, not in a challenging way, but with genuine curiosity.

It was Babette, finally, who found her voice. "Prithee . . . eh . . . my liege. On your kindness we do rest," she said. Bridget and Barnaby looked at their friend with alarm. "We came to Elsinore quite by accident, with none but the most innocent ends in mind, and **abide** here with only friendliness in our hearts."

Hamlet turned back to his skull. He touched the top of it gently with an index finger. "Came ye by sea?" he asked. "Your speech is fine, but soundeth tinged with **Gallic** cadence. Are you French?"

"I am, my lord," Babette said.

"Then you came by land," Hamlet concluded. "But my worthy soldiers found you with no mounts beneath you. Have you traveled all this way afoot?"

Babette looked down at the stone floor of the chamber and hesitated. "We came, sir, by a conveyance unknown to you in this time and place," Babette went on. "We would gladly tell you of it, were it not to strain your trustfulness." Hamlet stared the French girl down, somehow willing her to continue. "It is a sort of magic."

The prince's stare turned visibly colder. He took his hand away from the skull.

"Marcellus, Barnardo," he said. "Faithful servants: leave me with these prisoners. I would speak with them in confidence."

"As you wish, my lord," Marcellus said, stepping forward. "But I do not like to—though they appear pitiful, bedraggled, and weak, I fear they have trickery at their hands."

"Do not worry," Hamlet said, standing up and looking the kids over. "I have of late known treachery so foul as to possess knowledge of it aforehand. I will not turn my back to them."

"We shall be within summoning distance," Marcellus replied, bowing. The two knights turned and left the chamber.

When their footsteps faded, the silence that followed seemed to last a very long time. Hamlet looked toward the kids but not exactly at them. His eyes seemed far away. The kids held perfectly still. All at once, Hamlet squeezed his eyes shut and shook his head, then turned and charged back to the window. He stayed there, with his back to the room.

"You speak of magic," he said, "and I must by rights accept your testimony. For I myself, upon that very parapet"—Hamlet gestured to window and the battlement outside it—"encountered a vision of the dead, as like the man in life as you are standing now before me."

"Your father," Babette said. She couldn't help herself.

Hamlet turned quite slowly to face her. His face twitched.

"Not only do you come to Elsinore by supernatural means," he said softly, "but you practice black arts yourselves." More forcefully, he inquired: "How know ye t'was my father's ghost I sighted?"

"'Tis known widely, my lord," Babette replied, throwing caution to the wind. "We know of your lordship's kindness and sensitivity even where we hail from, and we come to Elsinore to beg your assistance in our quest."

Hamlet paused a moment, then waved his hand. "Bah!" he exclaimed. "Couldst I make myself an agent of your travails when so much evil haunts my country and its throne? I hardly have the leisure to be useful to a pack of **leery** strangers, however nobly they may speak of me to dull my senses in their favor."

Bridget spoke up: "But, sir! Um . . . lordship. Our cause is yours . . . is thine, indeed. Banish us from your kingdom if it is not!"

Hamlet smiled bitterly. "'Tis not my kingdom, child," he corrected her. "Wearing my father's crown, seated upon his throne, is the murderous scoundrel who saw him dead." Hamlet wheeled back to the window and pounded on its sill with his fist. "Pestilence!" the prince thundered.

"Whatever," Bridget whispered.

"Please, lordship," Babette said, "let us tell you of our plight. Surely hearing the object of our long, relentless journey will bring you to sympathy and to action."

Hamlet, head bowed at the window, reached out to touch the skull next to him. "Alas, poor Yorick," he said raggedly to the skull. "Would that I could lose myself in thine outrageous revels and infinite jest. The sky is uncommon dark of late, the fog declines to lift, and laughter is all but lost in the state of Denmark." The prince turned back to Babette and looked at her tiredly. "Tell me of your problem," he said. "Let it occupy my thoughts awhile and I'll be grateful to you."

Babette, with Bridget's help, told the prince their story: the world that they had traveled from, Wallet Fence's power to whittle Hamlet's world down to a puny version of itself, and their desperation not to let it happen. Hamlet listened, first sitting at the window seat, then getting up to pace the room, and finally returning to gaze at the skull of Yorick, the court jester who had been his friend when he was a child.

"What maketh a tyrant?" Hamlet asked when the kids' story was finished. "The will to punish humankind is ever abroad in the land. Indeed, it has weighed so heavily upon my head of late."

"We hoped you would have an idea," Babette said, "a method we could use to thwart this evil plan."

"Hmm," the prince mused. "Were thee to counter madness thou must be mad thyself."

Barnaby spoke up finally. "But Fence isn't crazy," he said. "Just greedy."

"Ah!" Hamlet said. "Then his greed must be turned in on itself. He must be made greedy for beauty instead of gold, the full form of truth instead of the spindly skeleton of numbers, the superfluity of the peacock instead of the mortal bleakness of the crow . . ."

"Okay, okay!" Bridget interrupted. She was growing impatient with Hamlet's long speeches. "But how?"

The prince sat back down on the window seat, brought up short by Bridget's interruption and at a loss as to what response to make.

"How?" he repeated. "How, indeed? Yes. We must to **rumination** lend our weary heads. I have spent a **fortnight** doing little else. I should be well and truly in the practice of it." He fell silent and turned to Yorick's skull for inspiration. Finding none, he looked to the window, out into the great, white fog bank that seemed perpetually to cover the castle.

Finally, Hamlet turned back to the kids. "Let us venture to the wood, where we may take advisement from the spirits," he suggested. He nodded, as though to approve his own idea. "Yes, it is uncommon close and musty in this chamber. This problem needs the air to flush its secretive solution." With that, Hamlet picked up his sword belt and buckled it about his waist. The kids followed him to the door and down into the staircase.

Many of the people gathered in the courtyard when the kids had first been brought in were still there. Some had left and been replaced by others. All who noticed Hamlet passing bowed their heads as he went by, and each of them stared at the kids with surprise.

The Prince of Denmark and his three visitors strolled out of the castle walls and down the hill toward the woods. Hamlet said nothing until they reached the tree line. There he stopped and looked back at the grand castle, shrouded in fog. The kids stopped too, and stood watching Hamlet.

"'Tis in this place that my mind has been most productive," he told them. "Now, what is the problem? A powerful man seeks to remake the world in his own horrid **visage**. There is no rebellion but your own small efforts. How does the mighty Goliath fall? What are his weaknesses? How can he be pained, frightened, influenced to the Good? These are seedlings we must tend well for a healthy plan to sprout."

"But what if he has no weakness?" Babette asked.

"Every man hath a weakness," the prince replied. "You have said his judgment is addled by greed. Mayhap that's his Achilles heel. A lust for power, a single person he hopeth to impress. One of these he must have."

"We don't know Fence very well," Bridget said. "All we know is he wants his computers to replace books and he doesn't care if all the books are ruined."

"Then he must be made to care," Hamlet said. "You've told me you have magic at your disposal. Why not concoct some spell to turn his thoughts around?"

"We don't know how to *use* magic," Babette told him. "We were shown the Continuum and that's all the magic we have."

"Hmm, I see," Hamlet said. He looked up at the treetops and breathed deeply. "I suppose poison is out of the question, though many a problem hath been addressed by its use."

"No, we can't poison him," Bridget said.

"Of course," Hamlet said. "'Twould only lead to greater woe; 'twas merely a suggestion, issued in the main to rule it out. So!" Hamlet, shifting his gaze to the ground, turned and began walking deeper into the woods. "Magic—nay. Poison—nay. Reason? Can a tyrant be reasoned with? It seemeth by design to be a foolish thought; for if reason itself be so foreign to a man's mind, how may it be introduced at such a late date?"

Hamlet was striding along at a fairly quick pace, so that the kids had to trot to keep up. The prince didn't look where he was going, but still somehow avoided colliding with the grim-looking trees. "Blast!" he said to the ground as he walked. "This problem is so **vexing**! How does one meet the will to destroy except with force of arms? That's it!"

"What?" Bridget asked breathlessly.

"If this man would destroy he must be destroyed—it is the best part of persuasion," Hamlet said. He looked pleased.

Bridget was confused. "But we already told you: we can't use force. Where we come from we would go to jail for it. Besides, it's wrong."

"Wrong!" Hamlet said bitterly. "And what is this Fence's action?"

"'Twould only lead to greater woe,'" Babette broke in. "Those are his lordship's own words, as he may recall, spoken just moments ago."

"Pestilence!" Hamlet exclaimed. "You unman me with my own weapon. I am a humble knight indeed."

The prince stood dejected in the middle of a clearing. A few feet away there was a well made of stone and wood. A bucket tied to a rope sat on the edge of the well. "This dilemma will drive me madder even than my uncle, the wrongful king, thinks me." Hamlet turned to the kids. "It grows late," he said, "and I find myself hungry for the first time in an eon. Would you, my guests, for you be no longer prisoners, care to join me for an early **sup**? We could dwell further on your problem over venison."

"Actually, your lordship," Bridget began. "We really should begin our journey home."

"Very well then," Hamlet replied. "If it's horses you require, I can have a trio of fresh mounts ready and at your disposal at the tolling of the hour."

"We have no such need," Babette told the prince, "though your lordship is very kind to offer. The Continuum should deposit us at home without the help of horse power."

"Ah! So you said," Hamlet recalled. "Well, then. Go you with speed and care! Do not rest until your mission is complete."

"We shan't, my lord," Babette promised.

Hamlet set off for the castle through the dusky fog, muttering to himself and staring at the ground.

"Well, he was a big help," Bridget said. "Yak, yak, yak—and all he could come up with was poisoning Wallet Fence!"

Babette was unshaken in her opinion of the prince. "Some of what he said was good," she said.

"Like what?" Bridget wanted to know.

"Like," Babette began, pausing. "Like making Fence care about beauty."

Right," Bridget said. "That should be a snap. If he doesn't care about ruining all the books, there's no way we can make him care."

"Maybe," Babette said sadly.

"Do you know what I care about?" Barnaby asked. "The same thing I've cared about since we started this wild goose chase. Getting back to New York! Now let's find the Continuum before it gets dark."

"You said it," Bridget replied. "Now where's that tree?" She looked around, then wobbled a little. "Hey!" she exclaimed, looking down, for Beauregard had brushed against her legs. He was holding a stick in his mouth. "Beauregard! Where did you go?"

Without responding, Beauregard leapt up onto the ledge of the well in the middle of the clearing. Sitting still for a moment, he made sure that he had everybody's attention. Then he leaned over and dropped the stick into the well.

"What was that for?" Bridget asked.

"Wait a minute!" Barnaby said. "Listen."

"Listen to what?" Babette said.

"That's just it," Barnaby answered. "Nothing. There was no splash when that stick hit the water, which means there's no bottom to that well, which means . . ."

"The well is the door to the Continuum!" Bridget said.

"Let's go," Barnaby said.

The three kids lunged forward, but as they did, two figures stepped out of the trees. They were Fence's henchmen.

"Thank you for alerting us," Richardson said. "We weren't sure how we were going to get home."

"Oh, for goodness' sake!" Bridget said wearily. "You followed us here?"

"Of course," the man said, his flannel-garbed crony standing by.

"That was pretty slick, how you sent us here," Bridget admitted.

Richardson smiled. "Thanks," he said. "Where would you like to go now? *Willy Wonka's Chocolate Factory*? *The Wizard of Oz*?"

Bridget smiled back at him. "We're too old for those books," she said. "We'll just go home now. Thank you very much though." She climbed onto the wall and dangled her legs into the well. Babette and Barnaby climbed up too; they moved slowly, eyeing the two bespectacled men with caution.

"I'm afraid that's quite impossible," Richardson said.

"Look, we've had enough," Bridget told him. "We don't care anymore what Fence does. We just want to get back." She inched forward on the wall of the well and reached out for Babette's hand.

"We'd like to believe you," Richardson said. "But if you make one more move, I'll yell out Dante's *Inferno*. And you won't like it there."

"I swear," Bridget said. "We won't interfere in Fence's plans. He can turn all the libraries into hot dog stands for all we care."

"Now I *know* you're lying," Richardson said. He took a step forward.

Bridget slipped. Without meaning to, she fell forward into the well. Seeing her go, Richardson yelled out, "*Oz!*" But Bridget didn't fall.

Babette held onto Bridget's hand. Hooking her other arm over the wooden crossbeam above the well, Babette braced herself and pulled. The Continuum was trying to suck Bridget in, but Babette struggled, and Bridget held on to her friend for dear life.

"Help!" Bridget gasped. She could feel the pull, much stronger than gravity, that the Continuum was exerting. Her sneakers began slipping off.

"Don't let go!" Babette told her.

Finally, the stress on the other end started to abate, and Babette was able to haul her friend back to safety. Bridget fell over the wall and onto the hard-packed earth of the forest floor, and lay there a moment to catch her breath. Remembering that she was furious, she then jumped up and lit into Richardson.

"You cut that out!" she yelled. "I could've been hurt in *The Wizard of Oz*! There's a tornado in it!"

Richardson looked uneasy. He folded his hands together. "I was just doing my job," he said.

"That's no excuse," Bridget scolded. She got down off the wall. "Now, are you going to let us go, or do we have to resort to violence?" Ominously, Babette hopped off the wall too, landing behind Bridget and towering over her, peering at Richardson through her dark glasses.

Richardson took off his own spectacles. "I should warn you," he said. "I'm a green belt."

"Brown," Babette said, moving Bridget out of her way. Richardson gulped.

The sound of pounding hooves filled the clearing. The kids and their two **antagonists** looked up. It was Hamlet!

"What ho!" the prince cried. "I had another idea pursuant to your stubborn plight, but thought I'd find you gone. Yet here you still abide. Why should it be so?"

Babette glanced at Richardson, then went up to Hamlet's horse.

"Your lordship," she said. "We would **fain** be well upon our way, but the mischief of these two highwaymen hath delayed us."

"State your business!" Hamlet roared at the two men. Richardson jammed his glasses back onto his face, but couldn't think of what to say to Hamlet. "Right! If ye be evildoers t'will be determined in the privacy of Elsinore's dungeon." The prince drew his sword. "On your way!"

Fence's henchmen looked at one another.

Hamlet's horse reared. "I'll not invoke the authority vested in me by rule of law a second time," Hamlet said menacingly, "but will let my blade speak in my stead lest you defy me one moment longer!"

Richardson and his sidekick started walking ahead of Hamlet's horse. Babette tugged on the prince's sleeve. He bent down to hear her.

"If it please you, do not hurt them, my lord," she said. "They are agents of the tyrant we hath spoken of, but they be not evil men."

"I thought as well," Hamlet replied. "I shall hold them a day or two to put you safely on your way."

"Thank you," Babette said. Hamlet nodded and kicked his horse, which trotted after the two prisoners.

Babette turned back to her friends. "Let us go," she said. They climbed back onto the edge of the well and joined hands.

Bridget looked over at her friends. "I wonder what Hamlet's idea was," she said.

Babette looked up. "Maybe I should go after him," she suggested.

"No!" Bridget and Barnaby said in unison. The three friends looked down into the well.

"Think: *home*," Bridget reminded the others.

"We are," Barnaby said.

"One, two, three," Bridget counted. And they all leaned forward and dropped into the Continuum. Beauregard went last; he was tired of being landed on.

While your understanding of a regular reading assignment can be vastly improved by note taking and rereading, these methods will help you even more when you read Shakespeare. The Bard wrote in the English of his time (the sixteenth and seventeenth centuries), using a lot of words that aren't used anymore and making a lot of references to the Bible and Greek and Roman drama. He also wrote in poetic verse, following metric rules (which govern the number of syllables in a line) and rhyming schemes that almost nobody uses to tell a story these days.

Luckily, most editions of Shakespeare's plays come with glossaries and detailed explanations of his speeches. So, when you set out to analyze a passage in Shakespeare, you get a lot of help right there in the book. Still, when something isn't clear to you, go back and read it again, without checking the glossary first, if you can. Some of the words won't make sense, but you will find a wealth of information in lines that, at first glance, seem to be just a bit of harmless poetry. Pay attention to the punctuation as well; it can help you see where one thought ends and another begins.

✍ DRILL #8 ✍

Read this speech by Hamlet.

> To be, or not to be: that is the question:
> Whether 'tis nobler in the mind to suffer
> The slings and arrows of outrageous fortune,
> Or to take arms against a sea of troubles,
> And by opposing end them. To die, to sleep—
> No more—and by a sleep to say we end
> The heartache, and the thousand natural shocks
> That flesh is heir to! 'Tis a consummation
> Devoutly to be wished. To die, to sleep—
> To sleep—perchance to dream: ay, there's the rub,
> For in that sleep of death what dreams may come
> When we have shuffled off this mortal coil,
> Must give us pause. There's the respect
> That makes calamity of so long a life:
> For who would bear the whips and scorns of time,
> Th' oppressor's wrong, the proud man's contumely,
> The pangs of despised love, the law's delay,
> The insolence of office, and the spurns
> That patient merit of th' unworthy takes,
> When he himself might his quietus make
> With a bare bodkin? Who would fardels bear,
> To grunt and sweat under a weary life,

But that the dread of something after death,

The undiscovered country, from whose bourn

No traveler returns, puzzles the will,

And makes us rather bear those ills we have,

Than fly to others that we know not of?

Thus conscience does make cowards of us all,

And thus the native hue of resolution

Is sicklied o'er with the pale cast of thought,

And enterprises of great pitch and moment,

With this regard their currents turn awry,

And lose the name of action.

As you can see, there are a lot of outdated terms, but try reading it again, and see if some more of the meaning comes through.

To be, or not to be: that is the question:

Whether 'tis nobler in the mind to suffer

The slings and arrows of outrageous fortune,

Or to take arms against a sea of troubles,

And by opposing end them. To die, to sleep—

No more—and by a sleep to say we end

The heartache, and the thousand natural shocks

That flesh is heir to! 'Tis a consummation

Devoutly to be wished. To die, to sleep—

To sleep—perchance to dream: ay, there's the rub,

For in that sleep of death what dreams may come

When we have shuffled off this mortal coil,

Must give us pause. There's the respect

That makes calamity of so long a life:

For who would bear the whips and scorns of time,

Th' oppressor's wrong, the proud man's contumely,

The pangs of despised love, the law's delay,

The insolence of office, and the spurns

That patient merit of th' unworthy takes,

When he himself might his quietus make

With a bare bodkin? Who would fardels bear,

To grunt and sweat under a weary life,

But that the dread of something after death,

The undiscovered country, from whose bourn

No traveler returns, puzzles the will,

And makes us rather bear those ills we have,

Than fly to others that we know not of?

Thus conscience does make cowards of us all,

And thus the native hue of resolution

Is sicklied o'er with the pale cast of thought,

And enterprises of great pitch and moment,

With this regard their currents turn awry,

And lose the name of action.

Now try answering the following questions. If you're having trouble, check the glossary on page 125.

1. What is Hamlet arguing with himself about?
   a. whether he should try to overthrow his uncle, the king
   b. whether it is better to die than to live
   c. whether his bodyguards are conspiring against him

2. What conclusion does he come to?
   a. It is better to die than to live.
   b. It is better to live, because the afterlife may be even worse.
   c. Conflicting possibilities and overthinking make decision making too difficult.

3. What are some of Hamlet's examples of negative aspects of life?

    a. "the pangs of despised love" and "the whips and scorns of time"

    b. "the native hue of resolution" and "a bare bodkin"

    c. "the pale cast of thought" and "the undiscovered country"

4. At what point in this speech does Hamlet's logic turn around? When does he begin arguing for life instead of death?

    a. "For who would bear the whips and scorns of time . . ."

    b. "Thus conscience does make cowards of us all . . ."

    c. "ay, there's the rub . . ."

5. What does "this mortal coil" refer to?

    a. the body

    b. the earth

    c. clothing

The answers can be found on page 172.

Chapter Eight Glossary

abide (ə-bīd′) (v.)　remain, continue, stay

admonish (ad-män′ ish) (v.)　caution, advise, or encourage

afoot (ə-foŏt′) (adv., adj.) on foot, walking; in progress

antagonist (an-tag′ ə-nis′ tik) (n.)　opponent, adversary

astride (ə-strīd′) (adj.)　with a leg on each side of, straddling

audible (ô′ də-bəl) (adj.)　loud enough to be heard

bade (bād) (v., past tense of **bid**) commanded, ordered, directed

the Bard　William Shakespeare (bard) (**bard** is an old word for a poet)

battlement (bat′ l-mənt) (n.)　a parapet or cresting on a castle or building consisting of regularly alternating raised and lowered sections (crenels)

behead (bē-hed′) (v.)　to cut off the head

behoove (bē-hoōv′) (v.)　to be worthwhile to, as for personal profit or advantage

bourne (boōrn) (n.)　realm, region, domain

cajole (kə-jōl′) (v.)　to persuade by flattery or promises, wheedle

condensation (kän′ dən-sā′ shən) (n.) a condensed mass; the act or process of reducing a gas or vapor to a liquid or solid form

crony (krō′ ne)⁻　(n.)　an intimate friend or companion

dote (dōt) (v.) to bestow excessive love or fondness regularly (usually followed by *on* or *upon*)

doth (duth) (v.)   archaic form of **do**

eon (e′ än′) (n.)   a division of geologic time comprising two or more eras; (informally) a very long time

fain (fān) (adv.)   gladly, with pleasure

fortnight (fôrt′ nĭt′) (n.)   a period of two weeks

gainful (gān′ fəl) (adj.) valuable, capable of providing money

Gallic (gal′ ik) (adj.)   pertaining to the French or France

gloat (glōt) (v.) to look at or think about with great or excessive satisfaction

Goliath (gəlī′ əth)   the giant warrior, champion of the Philistine army, who David killed with a stone from a sling (biblical)

hail (hāl) (v.)   to have as one′s place of birth or residence (followed by *from*)

hath (hath) (v.)   archaic form of **have**

haunch (hônch) (n.)   the hip or fleshy part of the body about the hip

illustrious (i-lus′ trē-əs) (adj.)   highly distinguished, renowned, famous

importune (im′ pôr-tōōn′) (v.)   to beg for (something) urgently and persistently

invoke (in-vok′) (v.)   to call or pray for (as a deity or spirit); to declare to be binding

leery (lir′ ē) (adj.)   wary, suspicious (usually followed by *of*); (archaic) knowing, alert

marionette (mar′ ē-e-net′) (n.)   a puppet manipulated from above by strings attached to its jointed limbs

matchless (mach′ lis) (adj.) having no equal, peerless, incomparable

matriarch (mā′ tre ärk′) (n.) a woman holding a position analogous to that of a patriarch, as in a family or tribe

mayhap (mā′ hap′) (adv.) (archaic) perhaps (short for *it may hap*)

mount (mount) (n.) horse, or other animal, used or available for riding

odious (ō′ dē-əs) (adj.) deserving or causing hatred, hateful, repugnant, detestable

ominous (am′ ən-əs) (adj.) portending evil or harm, threatening

parapet (par′ ə-pet′) (n.) a defensive wall or elevation in a fortification

persuasion (pər-swā′ zhen) (n.) the act of persuading or seeking to persuade; the power to persuade

pince-nez (pans′ nā′) (n.) a pair of eyeglasses held on the face by a spring that pinches the nose

preside (prē-zĭd′) (v.) to occupy the place of authority or control, as in an assembly or meeting

prithee (prith′ ē) (interjection) (archaic) pray thee

pursuant (pər-soo′ ənt) (adj.) in agreement or conformity (usually followed by *to*)

quarry (kwôr′ ē) (n.) an animal or bird hunted or pursued; any object of search, pursuit, or attack

rumination (roo′ mə-nā shən) (n.) meditation, musing, pondering

shod (shäd) (adj.) wearing shoes

shroud (shrowd) (n.) a cloth or sheet in which a corpse is wrapped for burial; something that clothes or conceals like a garment

spire (spīr) (n.) a tall, acutely pointed pyramidal roof or rooflike construction upon a tower; a steeple

steed (stēd) (n.) horse

stint (stint) (n.) a limited, prescribed, or expected quantity; a share

thee (thē) (pron.) you (the objective case of **thou**)

thine (thīn) (pron.) yours (the possessive case of **thou**), that which belongs to thee

thou (thow) (pron.) (archaic) second person singular form of **you**

thwart (thwôrt) (v.) to oppose successfully, prevent from accomplishing a purpose

turret (tûr′ it) (n.) a small tower, usually one forming part of a larger structure, as of a castle or fortress

unbidden (un′ bid′ n) (adj.) not summoned, unwelcome

vacate (vā′ kāt′) (v.) leave, evacuate

venison (ven′ i-sən) (n.) the flesh of a game animal, such as a deer

vested (ves′ tid) (adj.) held completely, permanently, and inalienably

vestment (vest′ mənt) (n.) a garment, especially an outer garment

visage (viz′ ij) (n.) the face, especially of a human being, countenance

wrest (rest) (v.) to take away by force, to get by effort

Chapter 9
Home

My word. What a very lucky thing to have found that well. I feel my young companions owe me a meal or two for the number of times that I have managed to lead them out of danger. Naturally I am too polite to call the debt due explicitly. All I can do is hope that they honor it on their own initiative.

Elsinore was quite as I'd imagined it: wet, chilly, and ominous. It reminded me of certain portions of the Pacific Northwest, where I found myself once after falling asleep on a flatbed railway car. Imagine! I'd dozed off in the middle of one of Tabitha's wordier sentences—Tabitha was an acquaintance I'd made when I pulled into Whitefish, Montana, the week before. We were like two peas in a pod that week, and I thought very seriously about settling in Whitefish, which was my dear Tabitha's hometown. Anyway, we had sought refuge in the railroad yard after narrowly escaping a sticky situation in town, and were relaxing on the flatbed for awhile. Tabitha was a sparkling conversationalist, as am I. Indeed it was the thing that I found most appealing about her. But at the moment, I confess, I was very sleepy and wasn't really following her line of reasoning, which I believe concerned the benefits of life in the Great Plains states as opposed to what she imagined the Deep South had to offer. Tabitha was quite a booster of her territory. The Whitefish Chamber of Commerce would have done well to use her in its promotional materials. But, anyway, I guess I slipped into unconsciousness, and I guess this irritated my friend, for when I awoke I was quite alone, night had fallen, and the flatbed was moving! I didn't dare try to disembark, of course. There was nothing to do except wait until the next stop, which turned out to be Seattle, Washington. A fine town, but wet, chilly, and ominous in the very same way that Hamlet's princedom was, which is my point.

The fall through the Continuum, this time, seemed only moments long, shortened by the sweet knowledge that I and my companions would soon be home, at long last. However, at first, I wasn't at all certain that I *was* home, because the New York Public Library was not where I landed.

✐ ✐ ✐ ✐ ✐

Bridget was on her back this time, her body making an impression in the packed sand and gravel underneath her. Blinking in the glare of an overcast sky, she sat up and looked around. She seemed to be in the middle of a fenced-off scrap heap. The ground was littered with rusty debris, and the dilapidated buildings beyond the fence seemed uninhabited.

"Where are we?" she asked her friends. There was no response. She wheeled and looked behind her. "Babette? Barnaby? Where is everybody?"

She was quite alone. Brushing herself off, she reflected for a moment on her situation. Such reflection required a fresh piece of bubblegum, which she got from her jacket pocket. It was her last piece.

Chewing thoughtfully, Bridget walked across the lot to the fence surrounding it. "Let's see," she thought. "We jumped in the well, and then . . ." Reaching the fence, Bridget found a large sign near the exit. It said:

BROOKLYN NAVY YARD

"How did I get here?" she asked herself. "I should be in Professor Thorvaldson's office at the New York Public Library!" Then something horrible crossed her mind. "Oh no! What if Richardson had the wrong instructions? I could be in another novel!"

Leaving the Navy Yard, Bridget looked both ways at the empty street. "Maybe someone will come along who can tell me where I am."

As she walked up the little narrow street, she gained a certain familiarity with her surroundings. Bridget had been to Brooklyn many times, and the low, brownstone apartment buildings that she passed seemed to confirm that she was really in the borough that she remembered.

"Let's see," she said to herself. "If I can just find a subway station, I can be back in Manhattan in half an hour. Hopefully it isn't Sunday, and the library will be open."

As she walked, Bridget saw very few people or cars. Up ahead was a broad avenue, on which she hoped to see some sign of life and find someone to provide her with directions to the subway.

Before she got there, though, she received a big shock. Out of nowhere, a small boy appeared, a boy who seemed to be running for his life. One moment, he wasn't there, and the next he was.

And he was running straight at Bridget! She hadn't even time to move to the left or right before the boy plowed straight into her and they both went tumbling onto the sidewalk. The boy no sooner disentangled himself from Bridget than he was scrambling to his feet, attempting to get back to his wild escape from whatever was pursuing him.

"Hey!" Bridget yelled, outraged at the lack of even a mumbled apology. "What's the rush! How about an 'excuse me'?"

The boy looked stricken and came out with "PardonmemmissI'mverysorryI" and then stopped. Bridget gaped at him as she began to realize who he was. The frightened little face, the knickers and cap. The boy who had knocked her down was Oliver Twist himself!

"Oliver!" Bridget said in disbelief. "What are you doing here?"

"Bridget?" Oliver came back. "I was—why, I was bein' chased by the bobbies! They spotted me on the way to Mr. Brownlow's house and started wavin' their clubs at me so I ran. Then I fell down a big hole I didn't even know was there and fell for the awfullest long while! I was down on the pavement and dint know what was happenin' so I takes off again and—"

Bridget interrupted him. "Wait a minute," she said. "Slow down. You were chased by the bobbies? You mean the police?"

"Yes, miss," Oliver told her.

"And you fell in a hole?"

"Yes, miss, a big, scary hole," Oliver reiterated. "An' when I hit the ground I skinned my knee." He lifted his leg up and showed her the hole in his knickers.

"My goodness," Bridget said, for it was occurring to her that what had happened was something Professor Thorvaldson hadn't counted on. "There must be more than one entrance to the Continuum, and it must be able to suck fictional characters in too!"

Bridget turned to Oliver. "Listen to me," she said, grabbing the boy by the shoulders. "I know how to get you back to London, but you have to trust me."

Oliver nodded.

"Come on," Bridget said, beckoning the boy to follow her.

And the two kids walked up and down the streets of Brooklyn until they found a subway that would take them to Manhattan.

✎ ✎ ✎ ✎ ✎

Barnaby was lucky. The fall didn't hurt at all this time. But it was suitably frightening, because when he came to a stop he couldn't breathe very well. Flailing his arms and yelling, he fought against whatever was covering his face and wriggled around until he was able to come up for air.

"What's going on?" he demanded. "Professor! Bridget!" The words echoed in Barnaby's ears. He looked around. There was no one there. "Professor?" he said more quietly. He was in a low-ceilinged room with a row of large washing machines. Looking down, he surmised that he was lying in a large canvas bin, atop a huge pile of white linen. Heaving himself over the side of the bin, he got to his feet on the gray concrete floor of the room. Barnaby took one of the linen garments out of the pile and examined it. It was a lab coat very much like the one he always wore. Evidently, he was in a laundry room, but other than that he was at a loss. He looked around again and saw a door with a red sign above it, reading Exit.

When Barnaby stepped out the door he was in the bustle of a long corridor full of people—people hurrying to and fro with clipboards, pushing gurneys with other people lying on them, and barking strange instructions to each other in what was unmistakably medical jargon.

"It's a hospital!" Barnaby thought to himself. "But what am I doing here?"

Keeping his back against the wall to stay out of the way of the speeding gurneys and people, Barnaby inched down the corridor. He made sure to avert his eyes from the faces of the doctors and nurses and orderlies. He didn't want to appear out of place. Fortunately, though, everyone was too busy to notice him, so Barnaby straightened his shoulders and began walking, looking around for signs to tell him how to get out.

When he'd turned several corners without success, he suddenly came upon a gurney stopped in the corridor, off to the side, against the wall. On it was a young boy who was struggling mightily to get off of it but was being prevented by a burly young orderly.

"Listen, kid," the orderly was saying. "I don't wanna hafta strap you down." But the kid was still struggling, and the orderly was looking over his shoulder for help when Barnaby passed by, pretending not to notice.

"Hey, doc," the orderly called. Barnaby stopped and turned, scared out of his wits. "Could you give me a hand here? This kid's scheduled for surgery in a few minutes and he's bein' a little difficult about it." The man's voice was strained. The kid was putting up quite a fight.

Barnaby paused a moment, shocked that the orderly thought he was a real doctor. "It must be my lab coat," he thought to himself. He looked down at the boy on the gurney and nearly jumped out of his skin.

"Huck?" Barnaby said.

"Barnaby!" the boy yelled delightedly. It was Huck Finn. "My old sharpshooter friend! Hey, tell this grizzly I ain't gettin' no surgery!"

Barnaby looked at the orderly, who appeared confused.

"His chart says he needs an appendectomy," the man said.

"Let me see it," Barnaby replied, in what he hoped was an authoritative voice. Apparently it was. The orderly handed the chart over.

Barnaby looked at it, but it was all a blur. He was too nervous to read any of it.

"No, no," he said. "This is all wrong. This boy is my patient, and he was just here for some blood tests. I put him out here to wait out the wooziness from giving blood. He doesn't need any kind of surgery at all. His chart must have been mixed up with someone else's."

"Yeah, you big possum," Huck said to the orderly. The man stepped back and Huck sat up, rubbing his arms.

"I'm sorry, doc," the orderly said. "You gonna take responsibility for him?"

Barnaby nodded. "I'll take it from here. Thanks a lot."

The orderly looked spooked, believing that he'd made a blunder.

"That's okay," he said. "No hard feelings, kid?"

"I'll think on it," Huck said to the man, who shook his head and walked away.

Huck turned to Barnaby. "I never been gladder to see anyone in my whole life," he said. "They'd-a gutted me sure if you hadn't come along. I dint know you was a real doctor!"

"I'm not," Barnaby said. He helped Huck Finn off the gurney and they started walking along the corridor. "Huck, how did you get here?"

"Blamed if I know!" the boy said. "I was a-spyin' on a coupla rough characters what was hidin' out on a old riverboat. I thought they mighta had somethin' I could use, but their conversation was givin' me the shivers, all about a murder they done and what was they gonna do now, and I thought as I should get outta there right quick."

"Good move," Barnaby said.

"Thanks," Huck said. "Anyways, I was just easin' myself real slow into my canoe alongside, when I lost my footing and I knowed I was goin' into the river. But I dint. The darnedest thing, I jus' kep fallin'. I fell and fell and I dint know where I was, like fallin' out of a big tree in the dark!"

Barnaby finished for him. "And when you hit the ground it wasn't the ground."

"You got it!" Huck said. "I come to right on that table, with that big crazy feller holdin' me down."

Barnaby stopped. He'd spotted the hospital's front desk up ahead, and beyond it was a pair of swinging glass doors.

"Come on, Huck," Barnaby said. They walked through the lobby and out of the hospital.

Once they were out in the parking lot, Barnaby turned and looked up at the sign above the building's entrance. It read: Staten Island Hopital.

"Thank goodness," Barnaby said.

"What?" Huck asked. "You know where we are?"

"Yes," Barnaby said. "And if you come with me, I can get you back to Missouri."

"Sounds good to me," the boy said, slipping his thumbs under the straps of his overalls. "Lead the way."

Barnaby walked up to an ambulance parked in the driveway and asked its driver for directions to the ferry to Manhattan.

✎ ✎ ✎ ✎ ✎

Babette's sunglasses were **askew**, and she had a bad taste in her mouth. Reaching up to her face, she pulled a piece of paper away from her lips and looked at it. It was a twenty-dollar bill.

Shifting her sprawled body she looked down. She was lying on a pile of money in a grim little room lit by a row of garish fluorescent bulbs. Babette rolled off the pile and stared at it. It must have been thousands of dollars, wrapped in bundles of ones, fives, tens, and twenties, and piled about four feet high. Babette straightened her glasses and stood quietly for a moment, trying to figure out what kind of bizarre place she was in, and why she was alone. She hadn't long to wonder. Hearing a noise behind her, she turned to see a little man in a rumpled shirt and tie, his vest unbuttoned, coming through the door. The man was mostly bald and was wearing a visor on his head that was like a baseball cap without the part that covers your head. He looked up and saw Babette. A startled sound escaped him—somewhere between a cough and a gurgle. The French girl didn't hesitate. There was no way out of the room except over the man, who was flat on his back before he was able to shout, "Security! Rufus!"

As Babette left the visored man behind, she nearly ran into a giant of a uniformed security guard, who was standing just outside the door of the room. Deftly evading the man's waving arms, Babette kept running, not pausing to notice the crowd of people milling about and lined up in front of a row of little, glassed-in cubicles.

"Stop her, Rufus!" the first man cried in a high, scratchy voice. "She was in the counting room!"

Rufus was giving chase. Babette chose one of two alleyways leading out. She tore up the ramp and came out into daylight, distractedly hearing the roar of a large crowd. She ran down a flight of steps, past row upon row of people, some sitting in seats, some standing, yelling, weeping. Babette didn't look behind her. She could feel the big security guard on her tail, and had no idea how many were coming to his aid.

Reaching the bottom of the stairs, Babette came to a chest-high railing, which she jumped gracefully, without breaking stride, bracing herself with her right hand. Landing on dirt, she took off headlong for an identical railing several yards away, until something made her skid to a stop.

The roar of the crowd had gotten louder, but Babette heard a voice behind her, urging her hysterically to come back.

"Get off the track! You'll be killed!"

Babette turned and saw the security guard she had dodged. Then she looked to her right.

She was in the middle of a racetrack. There was a horse race in progress, and a mass of horses was bearing down on Babette so fast she hardly had time to think. All she could do was drop to a crouch, cover her head with her arms and hope against hope that none of the horses would trample her. The crowd's roar was deafening. The thunder of the horses' hooves pounded in Babette's ears, matching the furious racing boom of her heart.

Something saved her. At first, she didn't know what. All she knew was that her whole body was yanked up off the ground and that she was flying through the air, staring down at the blur of the dirt track. Then her body was hoisted in a flash, she was whipped around, and she came to rest on the back of a charging horse, a strong, deep voice sounding above the wind, the crowd noise, everything.

"Hold exceeding tight, milady!" the voice said. "There shan't be but a middling bump in store!"

Babette held onto the waist of the owner of the voice as hard as she could. She could barely peer over his shoulder, but she saw the railing, where the track curved, coming up fast. Then they were airborne, sailing over it. When they hit the ground, the horse kept galloping across a brief expanse of field. Jumping another, lower rail, the horse stumbled slightly. The animal was having trouble finding its footing on asphalt. Babette held on tighter, for approaching them from the right was a passenger bus. They were on a highway.

"Onward, brave stallion!" the man holding the reins cried. The horse whinnied, jumped another guardrail, and veered off to the left, along a broad median, coming to a rearing halt in a grove of trees. The three of them were still for a moment, apparently out of danger and definitely out of breath. Then the man looked over his shoulder at Babette.

"Propitious, indeed, that we should meet again thus," he commented. "Would you not say the same?"

It was Hamlet. Babette gaped at him as he dismounted and held a hand out to help her down.

"Thank you," the girl murmured, accepting his hand, though she meant to thank him for a great deal more than that. "I am surprised to see you again."

"Easily no more surprised than I am to find myself here," the prince replied. His horse had bent its head and was helping itself to some of the thick, green grass on the median. Hamlet and Babette sat on the ground, and he commenced to tell her how he had turned up on the racetrack. "I was out for a ride on the grounds of the castle, a brisk gallop to clear my head. My horse had just cleared the high hedgerow along the western edge of the wood near Elsinore."

"And you both kept falling," Babette guessed.

"Just as you say," Hamlet confirmed, looking up at her. "We fell perilously, tumbling through a blackness more profound than the depths of a moonless night. It was all I could do to **cleave** to my saddle, praying wildly, even profanely, that my mount would not land atop my body. How we ended in that arena, amongst those other knights, I will never know."

"I think I know," Babette told him. "You traveled through the Continuum that my friends and I told you about. I think you have somehow entered my world."

Hamlet laughed bitterly. "I shouldn't think that supernatural events would shock me so," he said, "given the tumult of recent weeks."

Babette stood and peered through the trees at the racetrack they had escaped from. Above the grandstand, she could make out a large sign that said Yonkers Raceway. The roar of the crowd was a faint sound above the traffic on the highway.

"Yonkers," Babette said to herself. She turned and looked down at Hamlet. "We are not so far from where we need to go to get you back to Elsinore," she told him. "Can your horse be ready soon?"

Hamlet nodded. "I should say he's had a goodly rest," the prince said. "I must to Elsinore to untangle the cursed king's web. And I expect your pursuers, bereft this very moment in Elsinore's dungeon, do verily await their reprieve."

Babette smiled. "Fence's henchmen? You have not used them harshly, I trust."

Hamlet helped her onto the horse. "No more so than any other minor thieves, though I may have led them to believe the executioner's hatchet doted on their scrawny throats."

The prince hoisted himself onto his horse and they galloped off, south toward Manhattan.

Beauregard, meanwhile, was having a hard time. Landing in the attic room of the Prospect Park boathouse, he had been chased around the offices there by the park rangers, found his way downstairs, and escaped to the bank of Lullwater Pond. Resting underneath the footbridge, he was just getting his bearings when he was set upon by a huge, snarling rottweiler, a breed of dog known for its particularly uncharitable and aggressive behavior toward cats. Making an educated decision to avoid a fight, Beauregard was forced to flee. The dog was young and energetic, and didn't tire easily. Beauregard did one lap around the lake, then decided to head for the nearest tree, up which the dog would not be able to follow him. He just managed to leap clear of the snapping teeth and alight on a branch high above the ground, from which he regarded the howling brute with monumental disdain, though his chest was heaving from his exertions.

"A city whose leash laws are so poorly enforced is not a city I can grace with my presence for very long," Beauregard thought to himself. The dog kept barking for a very long time, and Beauregard was afraid that its owner would never come to retrieve it. "Blah, blah, blah," the cat thought, mimicking his antagonist in his mind. "How long will I have to wait until this hysteric wears himself out? I must get to the library before it closes. Bridget will require my assistance." Sighing, Beauregard stretched out on the tree branch and gazed over the pond, trying to blot out the irritation of the dog's barking by concentrating on the calm water and the people maneuvering their paddleboats around and around. Noticing something on the pond, Beauregard narrowed his eyes and sat up. The occupants of one of the paddleboats looked very familiar: a finely dressed man and a teenage girl who was wearing a plain but old-fashioned dress.

"Jo March!" thought Beauregard, identifying the girl. "And that looks like the mysterious millionaire we met out at the beach. I wonder how they came to be in Prospect Park? Perhaps they'll appreciate it if I take them to Bridget." Beauregard stood up, glanced at the barking dog far below and walked out to end of the tree branch, which stretched out over the bank of the pond. The paddleboat came closer, closer . . .

"Why, it's that marvelous black cat who visited us back in Boston!" Jo March cried when Beauregard landed in the boat. Gatsby stopped peddling and held on to the side of the vessel, which was rocking rather violently under the force of Beauregard's arrival. The cat hopped immediately onto the seat between Jo and Gatsby, out of the way of the little puddle of water sloshing around the bottom of the boat.

"You two know each other?" Gatsby asked.

"Yes," Jo said. "He came with the children we were talking about, the ones who visited your estate."

"You don't say?" Gatsby replied, declining further comment.

The paddleboat, unpeddled, was drifting toward shore. The rottweiler being nowhere in sight, Beauregard chose that moment to disembark, jumping onto dry land and turning immediately back to Jo and Gatsby. He fixed them with a meaningful feline stare.

"Perhaps he can lead us to those children, and they can direct us back home!" Jo said hopefully.

"Nonsense," Gatsby said. "If I can get to a phone I'll just call my chauffeur and he'll come get me."

Jo gave Gatsby a shove. "Well, I can't summon *my* chauffeur, and if you got here the way *I* did, which you say you did, I'll wager that your *chauffeur* is unavailable."

"Wager, eh?" Gatsby said. He smiled his winning smile. "You may have a point. I suppose I'll tag along." Gatsby got out of the boat first and helped Jo out. "But, I say, isn't it rather common to just abandon the boat here without returning it?"

"Oh, be a dear and hush up about commonness," Jo said irritably. "You're simply obsessed!"

Gatsby frowned and put his hands in his pockets. "Look," he said, "your friend has a bit of a start on us." Jo looked and saw that Beauregard had headed off toward the edge of the park.

"Hurry!" Jo said, gathering up her long skirts to keep from tripping. "We must catch up to him!"

Out on the street, Gatsby had to grab Jo's arm to keep her from running into traffic in pursuit of Beauregard.

"Careful, old sport," he warned. "You'll be slaughtered by them automobiles."

"Automobiles?" Jo said, looking around the Brooklyn streets in wonder. "Why, I've never seen anything like them!"

"They are rather modern, aren't they?" Gatsby said. "Must be new models. I'll tell my man to pick one up for me."

Crossing Grand Army Plaza from the edge of the park, Gatsby and Jo found Beauregard waiting patiently at the top of the subway station steps. When he saw that they had seen him, the cat bounded down the stairs and under the turnstile. The humans, of course, had to stop and buy tokens.

"A dollar-fifty!" Gatsby said with alarm when he saw the sign. "The subway was a nickel the last time I checked." He looked thoughtful. "Of course, that was a very long time ago."

Jo pulled on his arm. "Yes, and you're a blindingly wealthy man and all that," she said impatiently. "Do hurry or we'll lose him!"

Gatsby paid and the two of them went through the turnstile and down the stairs, where they found Beauregard sitting on a bench, waiting for the train to Manhattan.

On Fifth Avenue, outside the New York Public Library, everything was just as it had been the last time Bridget climbed the library steps. It was still Saturday; Bridget had confirmed that by asking the token clerk in the subway station. The avenue was fairly busy; the library steps were adorned with people lounging, eating lunch, and generally enjoying the weather. Bridget looked up and down the avenue.

"Darn it," she said. "I was hoping Babette and Barnaby would be here by now. I'm sure they're on their way. Unless something's happened to them." She looked down at Oliver, who was staring around at the cars and buses as though he expected them to jump the curb and run him down. "Oh," Bridget said, smiling. "I forgot you'd never seen cars before."

"How do they move without horses to pull them?" Oliver asked.

"They each have something called an engine, which runs on gasoline," Bridget told him. "I'd explain how it works, but I don't really know myself. Maybe Barnaby will tell you later. Hey! Here he comes now."

Barnaby came hurrying down the street in spurts, having to keep stopping to retrieve a **recalcitrant** Huck, who just wanted to gape at the buildings, cars, and crowds of people.

When they arrived in front of the library, Bridget greeted them happily. "Welcome back, Barnaby! I see you had the same experience as me."

"I hope not, for your sake," Barnaby said. "I practically had to restrain Huck from jumping off the Staten Island Ferry. He was a little spooked when we pulled into Manhattan. Shall we go in?"

"We should wait for Babette," Bridget reminded him. "I was hoping she'd be with you."

At the mention of their friend's name, the sound of horse's hooves sounded up the avenue. The sound grew louder as the horse galloped toward them. The friends and their two fictional charges turned around to see Hamlet's impressive steed slowing to a stop.

"Whoa, stallion," the prince yelled. "And, ho, fine friends! I see my passenger did not point me hither undutifully." Babette and Hamlet dismounted, just as Beauregard, Gatsby, and Jo arrived.

"Jo and Mr. Gatsby!" Bridget said. "It's good to see you again!" She looked down at Beauregard, who was acknowledging the lion statue beside the library steps. "Good work getting them here."

"Hello, Bridget!" Jo cried. "He was most insistent that we follow him."

"Good," Bridget said. "Now that we're all here, please come with me. I want you to meet the man who will get you all home."

"Is it sound of law to tie my mount up here?" Hamlet inquired. "I should like to acquire a bag of oats for him to eat. He hath brought us very far and must be hungered."

"Oats?" Barnaby repeated. No one knew where to get oats of course.

Bridget thought a moment and then spotted a hot dog stand. "Will a pretzel do?" she asked the Danish prince.

"Pretzel?" Hamlet inquired. "I have not heard of such a victual, though if it be grain or grasses based, I cannot see the harm."

"It's sort of a salty bread," Bridget told him. "Babette, do you have any money? I'm broke." Babette shook her head.

Jo broke in, touching Gatsby's shoulder. "My gentleman here is positively weighed down with currency. Mr. Gatsby, could you spare the horse a pretzel?"

Gatsby took his billfold from the inner pocket of his well-tailored coat. "I suppose the price of pretzels has soared to ten dollars or so."

"Nope," Bridget told him. "They're just a dollar, maybe a little more."

Hamlet bowed to Gatsby. "I am indebted to you, good sir. Had I thought to bring my usual traveling budget of *krone*, I could reimburse you immediately. As the situation has it, I'm not sure when fair restitution I can make."

"Don't mention it," Gatsby said, and walked over to the hot dog stand.

"Bring your horse up on the sidewalk," Bridget said to the prince. "We'll tie him to the No Parking sign over there."

The woman at the information desk was startled to see Barnaby and Bridget walking toward her.

"Here to see Professor Thorvaldson again?" she asked. "I thought you were still down there with him! I guess I just didn't see you leave." Neither Bridget nor Barnaby told her that they had left from a different, very different, exit.

"Time seems to have stood still while we were gone," Barnaby observed as they led their entourage to the stairs. "Fascinating. I'll have to discuss that phenomenon at length with the professor."

"It seems to me that we know a lot more about the Continuum now than he does," Bridget said.

In the library's basement, all was quiet from the other side of Professor Thorvaldson's office door. Bridget knocked. There was no answer. She knocked again.

"Professor Thorvaldson?" she said, turning the knob. "We're back! And you'll never guess what happened!"

Bridget was brought up short when she entered the room by the sight of Professor Thorvaldson sitting in his desk chair, trussed up and gagged.

"Professor!" cried Bridget and Barnaby in unison, running to him with Babette and the others just behind them.

Professor Thorvaldson looked down at his desk and closed his eyes in defeat, just as the door slammed shut.

Everybody wheeled around to see three men standing there, revealed by the closing of the door. The man in the middle, the slightest of build, was a dead ringer for the photograph Professor Thorvaldson had hanging on his dartboard.

It was Wallet Fence III.

"Good afternoon," Fence said, in a gentle, rather high voice. "It's a pleasure to finally meet such brave adventurers. I've been worried that you would never find your way back."

"You could've fooled us," Bridget said. "Your two henchmen did everything they could to prevent us from getting home."

"Simply a delaying tactic, I assure you," Fence said. He didn't smile or roll his eyes in a villainous manner. In fact, the man seemed as shy and harmless as a child, right down to his boyish haircut and large eyeglasses. "They meant you no harm. I had to buy time until my lawyers and accountants could work out the purchase of all the publication rights that I needed for my plan to work."

"Time?" Barnaby said. "But hardly any real time has passed since we entered the Continuum."

"That's true," Fence said. "Only a few hours have gone by in the real world, but that's all my people needed. The process was well under way when the news of my press conference appeared in the newspapers. I had hoped that Richardson and Bell would delay you a few days more, but you managed to elude them. I should congratulate you for that, but maybe you could tell me where they are."

"Those names are beknownst to me," Hamlet said, stepping in front of Bridget. "The men to whom they belong languish this very hour in the dungeon at Elsinore!"

"Wallet Fence, meet Hamlet, the prince of Denmark," Barnaby said.

"Um, pleased to meet you," Fence said.

"Would that I could say the same," the prince replied.

"When you return to your world, I'd appreciate it if you set them free," Fence said. "Apart from being employees, they're also friends of mine."

"Then in their names and for their sakes you will desist from your reprehensible action!" Hamlet insisted.

"Hmm," Wallet Fence mused. "I see we have a problem. Well, maybe they'll be happy in Elsinore. In any case, my project will proceed as scheduled. There's a lot riding on it. Compucon must stay ahead of its competitors at all costs."

"I say, old sport," Gatsby piped up. "It's awfully uncouth of you to be so stubborn."

"You simply can't destroy all the books," Jo March added. "It isn't right."

"People will get used to it," Fence said. "People can get used to anything when they have no choice."

"I have made a choice," Hamlet replied, drawing his sword. "At long last."

The sound of the steel blade being pulled from its scabbard rang through the musty basement room. Everybody except Hamlet and Fence flinched. Fence's two bodyguards reached into their suit jackets and produced automatic pistols.

"No, Hamlet!" Bridget shouted, leaping in front of the prince. "They have guns!"

"What, those little, blunt instruments?" Hamlet scoffed. "Do they propose to hit me about the head and shoulders with them until I capitulate? Stand aside!" He took Bridget's shoulder and moved her away.

"Um, Hamlet, old sport," Gatsby interjected. "I believe she's right."

Hamlet paused, his sword at the ready, his eyes shifting from one bodyguard to the other. "She is?" he said.

"Yes," Jo told him. "Guns can kill from a distance, while your sword cannot."

"I begin to believe you," the prince said. He dropped his sword on the floor and knelt on one knee, bowing his head. "Your worthy soldiers have unmanned me, sir. Do your worst."

Babette took Hamlet at his word. Leaping forward and vaulting off the prince's back, she grabbed an overhanging heating pipe and swung her body forward, catching each of the bodyguards full in the face with her kicking feet. The men were so taken by surprise that they didn't manage to squeeze off so much as a shot from their pistols. Hamlet dove for one of the sprawling men, Gatsby for the other. Babette dropped gracefully to the floor, landing on her feet. When Fence stood up from his self-protective crouch, his bodyguards were disarmed, lying on their backs, covering their injured faces with their hands. Gatsby was training his automatic on one of the men, while Hamlet fumbled with the other gun, trying to figure out how to hold it.

"Careful with that gun, Hamlet!" Bridget warned.

Hamlet turned toward her holding the gun upside down. Everybody ducked, except Professor Thorvaldson, who would've if he hadn't been tied up.

"You have such facility with your weapon, sir," Hamlet said to Gatsby.

"Well, I was a lieutenant in the war," Gatsby explained.

"I reckon I got some 'sperience with a pistol," Huck Finn said, stepping forward. "Maybe y'oughter pass that off to me 'fore you hurt somebody, prince."

"I must concede your point, young sportsman," Hamlet said, handing the gun to Huck, who pointed it at Fence's other bodyguard.

Professor Thorvaldson, straining against the ropes, was trying mightily to speak, but his voice was muffled by the gag. Barnaby, standing behind his chair, took the gag from his mouth.

"A-ha!" the professor cried. "Seems as though the shoe is on the other foot now, Fence!"

Wallet Fence did not seem ruffled. "I commend your presence of mind," he said, nodding to Babette. He then looked up at the assembled crowd. "But I don't see how this turn of events serves your cause. My project goes forward, no matter what you do with me."

"Not if you call it off," Bridget corrected him.

Fence blinked myopically at her. "And how do you propose to induce me to do that?" he asked. "Threats? I am not susceptible to threats."

"We've got a wildcard," Bridget replied, turning and walking back to Professor Thorvaldson's desk. Barnaby was almost finished untying the professor's bonds.

"You'd better tie the three of them up," she said.

"What's our wildcard?" Barnaby whispered.

"Our last chance," Bridget said, reaching into her jacket pocket and pulling out an old, creased scrap of paper. It was Huck's friend Jim's magic spell.

"Is that everything?" Bridget asked, when Professor Thorvaldson returned from the library's upstairs exhibition rooms. Fence and his bodyguards were tied up and seated in the middle of the floor, their backs to one another, forming a three-point star. They were surrounded by lit candles, and the overhead lights had been turned out. The kids and their fictional companions sat here and there about the room, looking at the flickering shadows cast upon each other's faces. Beauregard reclined on a high shelf, observing all of them.

"I think so," the professor said, his arms full of strange items. "I found the snakeskin and bobcat tooth in the Teddy Roosevelt exhibit. The mustard seed and rose petals were easy: I just went to a delicatessen."

"Okay," Bridget said. "Give me the bobcat tooth. I have to hold it while I read the spell. Sprinkle the mustard seed in a circle around the prisoners. Then sprinkle the rose petals on top of the mustard seed."

Professor Thorvaldson started sprinkling, giggling as he went. "Right you are!" he wheezed through his giggles.

"For a man of letters," Fence observed, "you seem to be taking this hokum rather to heart."

At that, the old professor paused in his duties and leaned toward Fence, bringing his weathered, old face close to the computer tycoon's own.

"If it works," he said, smiling, "the world will be rid of your evil plan." The professor laughed, his mouth wide open, and commenced sprinkling.

When he was finished, Bridget consulted the scrap of paper again. She looked up.

"Now light the snakeskin on fire from a candle and lay it in front of Fence."

"What an awful stench," Jo March said, crinkling her nose when the snakeskin caught fire. Thick, acrid, white smoke rose from the burning skin toward the ceiling.

"Everybody repeat after me," Bridget said, looking down at the paper. She read, "All the faces of our kin . . ."

Her friends, the professor, Gatsby, Jo, Oliver, Hamlet, and Huck all repeated the words.

"All the faces of our kin . . ."

"and the pleading voices of their souls . . ." Bridget continued.

"and the pleading voice of their souls . . ." the group repeated.

"do lead us now through dark and din . . ."

"do lead us now through dark and din . . ."

"to quiet pastures, safely home . . ."

"to quiet pastures, safely home . . ."

The poem went on, through many stanzas, and the kids' and their new friends' voices filled the darkened room as one voice. Wallet Fence III watched the smoke rise from the smoldering snakeskin, and his eyeglasses reflected the candlelight as he fell into a trance.

✎ ✎ ✎ ✎ ✎

The following day, Bridget's parents had Barnaby and Babette over for lunch. When it was over, the adults left to go to a movie, and the three friends were left to entertain themselves. All of their fictional charges had been safely returned to their fictional worlds, though there had been some difficulty convincing the library authorities to let Hamlet's horse into the building. And then squeezing him through the hole in the basement office's wall was nearly impossible! But they managed, and now they were all back to lounging around, waiting for Monday, the first day of school. Except for Beauregard. He had taken leave of his human charges the evening before and set off on a visit to South Carolina.

When they left for the movie, Bridget's parents had picked up the newspaper from outside their front door and left it on the dining room table. Babette picked it up and brought it to the living room, where Bridget and Barnaby were watching TV.

"There's an article about Fence's press conference on the front page," Babette told them.

"It's on all the networks, too," Bridget said. "It looks like the spell worked."

The headline blared:

Wallet Fence Abandons Book-buying Spree

Computer Tycoon Retiring to Pursue "Other Interests"

New York, 21 September–Wallet Fence III, who only yesterday announced his plan to single-handedly change the traditional format of world literature, made an abrupt about-face this morning in a hastily called follow-up press conference. His new plan is to rescind the old plan completely and, in the process, quit the computer business. The high-tech industry was stunned by the announcement.

Fence expressed surprise at the widespread shock.

"I don't see what everyone's so surprised about," the billionaire said. "Can't a guy change his mind?"

Having spent literally hundreds of millions of dollars to acquire the rights to all the fiction and nonfiction works ever written, Fence has decided to return all of the copyrights he had purchased to their previous owners, while not demanding the immediate return of his investments.

"It's only money," Fence said simply, a shy smile spreading across his face.

When asked what he would do now, the one-time purveyor of computers, software, and Internet-access applications said he would like to become involved in the theater and had already applied to several drama study programs.

"I hope one of them accepts me," he said. "I've never acted before."

Mr. Fence was not prepared to answer further questions, he said, because he was late for a reading of a play that he was participating in at a friend's loft apartment. When a reporter fired off one last question, Mr. Fence relented and came back to the podium.

"What play are you reading?" was the question.

"*The Mahábhárata*," Mr. Fence replied. The auditorium fell silent as the reporters scribbled in their notebooks and turned to one another, mouthing the play's title.

The Mahábhárata is an ancient text from India, concerning the creation of the world and issues of bravery, love, and tragedy. Performed, it runs approximately nine hours.

"It's my favorite play," Mr. Fence added.

Babette finished the article and turned to the back of the paper to continue reading in her usual fashion. Bridget changed the channel to another station. The Yankee game was just starting. The three friends sat together and the murmur of the television mingled with the sounds of the traffic out on the street.

Any book you read will employ what are called plot devices, tools to move the story along, motivate the characters, and get them from one place to another. In this story, the Fiction–Reality Continuum is one plot device. It allows the kids to meet some of their favorite characters from literature and have adventures. (Can you think of any characters from the books you have read who you would like to meet if they were real people?) The magic spell the kids use to change Wallet Fence into a man who appreciates literature is another plot device. Even Wallet Fence himself is a plot device; after all he is the villain, the reason the kids have to go on an adventure.

When you are reading a book for which you will be expected to remember the important ideas, characters, and events it is helpful to be aware of the plot devices. Whenever you come across a plot device, you can say, "A-ha! Sooner or later something's going to happen that will make this significant." The notes you are taking as you read will make spotting the plot devices easier.

✍ DRILL #9 ✍

Here are some questions relating to chapter nine. See if you can answer them without going back to reread.

1. What was the name of the female cat Beauregard met in Whitefish, Montana?
   a. Rayette
   b. Agnes
   c. Tabitha

2. When Barnaby discovers Huck Finn in the hospital, what kind of unnecessary operation does he save the boy from?
   a. an appendectomy
   b. a tonsillectomy
   c. a lobotomy

3. What is the best word to describe Jo's attitude toward Gatsby?
   a. respectful
   b. sarcastic
   c. resentful

4. When the kids finally meet Wallet Fence, how would you describe his behavior?
   a. mean and unfriendly
   b. erratic, crazy
   c. mild but stubborn

5. What does Fence want to do with his life when the story ends?
   a. help others
   b. become an actor
   c. read a lot

The answers can be found on page 172.

Chapter Nine Glossary

acrid (ak' rid) (adj.) having an unpleasant smell or taste

adorn (ə-dôrn') (v.) decorate, drape on

appendectomy (ap' ən dek tə mē) (n.) operation to remove the appendix

askew (ə-skyoo') (adj.) at a strange or abnormal angle, crooked

bereft (bə rəft') (adj.) lacking anything, or (used with *of*) one specific thing

bobbies (bäb' ēz) (n.) slang for British police officers

booster (boost' tər) (n.) proponent, promoter

borough (bûr' ō) (n.) province or section of a place or city. New York has five: Manhattan, Brooklyn, Bronx, Queens, and Staten Island

bustle (bus' əl) (n.) an atmosphere of frantic activity, as in the movement of a crowd

capitulate (kə pich' yoo lāt') (v.) give up, give in, surrender

cleave (klēv) (v.) stick (to), or, sometimes, split (from)

commend (kə mend') (v.) praise, honor

concede (kən-sēd') (v.) admit, agree to

desist (di-sist') (v.) stop, discontinue a wrongful act

dilapidated (də lap' ə-dat') (adj.) run down, falling apart

din (din) (n) considerable noise, unreasonable loudness

disembark (dis' em-bärk') (v.) get down, get off (as in a train)

dutiful (do͞ot′ i-fəl) (adj.) obedient, proper, considerate

exceed (ek-sēd′) (adv.) (old-fashioned) exceedingly

facility (fə-sil′ ə-tē) (n.) dexterity, agility, grace

flail (flāl) (v.) thrash about, wave

hokum (hōk′ əm) (n.) nonsense, sentimental foolishness

hysteric (hi-ster′ ik) (n.) one who is hysterical or taken with hysteria, a crazy person

initiative (i-nish′ ə-tiv) (n.) the inclination or idea to do some action

jargon (jär′ gən) (n.) language, especially that specific to a trade; slang or argot

languish (lan′ gwish) (v.) waste away

monumental (man′ yo͞o-ment′ l) (adj.) important, large or extreme

myopic (mi′ äp′ ik) (adj.) nearsighted, (sometimes) unimaginative

ominous (am′ ən-əs) (adj.) frightening; symbolic of a bad omen; portent of doom

profane (prō-fān) (adj.) unholy, not hallowed or consecrated

propitious (prō-pish′ əs) (adj.) fortunate, good

purveyor (pər′ vā′ ər) (n.) provider, salesman

recalcitrant (ri-kal′ si-trənt) (adj.) hard to handle or deal with

refuge (ref′ yo͞oj) (n.) safety or hiding; a place to be safe or hide

reprehensible (rep′ ri-hən′ sə-bəl) (adj.) horrible, vile, unworthy of sympathy or forgiveness

reprieve (ri-prēv′) (n.) postponement of punishment

rescind (ri-sind′) (v.) take away

restitution (res′ tə-tōo′ shən) (n.) repayment

scabbard (skab′ ərd) (n.) sheath or holster for a sword

smolder (smōl′ dər) (v.) to burn and smoke without flame

stricken (strik′ ən) (adj.) afflicted or affected, as by something very distressing

supernatural (sōo′ pər-nach′ ərəl) (adj. or n.) existing or occurring outside the natural experience of man, involving the occult

trussed (trus′ d) (adj.) tied (used with *up*)

tumult (tōo′ mult′) (n.) noise, commotion, or uproar

verily (ver′ əlē) ′ (adv.) (old-fashioned) in very truth, truly

victual (vit′ l) (n.) food or other provisions

Chapter 10
Comprehension and Vocabulary Drills

Here are some more exercises to help you sharpen your comprehension skills and test your vocabulary.

✍ PASSAGE #10A ✍

Find a straightedge (a ruler, a postcard, whatever) and use it to read the following passage, holding the straightedge under each line as you read.

Bridget got up in plenty of time to make it to school early on Monday, but, as was generally the case, something happened between the time she got out of bed and when she left the apartment. Time seemed to disappear. While eating breakfast, she looked at the sports section of the paper, reading three articles about the Yankees' Sunday afternoon loss to the Brewers. The loss, Bridget ranted to her mother, was inconceivable. And the commentary in the sports section didn't shed any light on it, either. Perhaps, dwelling on the defeat, Bridget lost her appetite, and spent more time reading than eating. Finally, Bridget's mother took her half-eaten bowl of cereal away (Bridget barely noticed) and ordered her into the shower.

Bridget knew she was not a very efficient bather. She had good hygiene, of course, but it took her awhile to get clean. First, she needed to stand under the water for a few minutes to get used to it; then she had to shampoo and condition her hair, letting first the shampoo and then the conditioner stay in her hair for a few moments while she lathered her arms and legs. The shower was also a place to think. Whose class would she be assigned to today? Would Babette have the same lunch period as she? How could the Yankees' Manager Joe Torre leave Jorge Posada in to hit in the bottom of the ninth inning when Mike Stanley was on the bench?

Finally, her shower finished, Bridget went into her bedroom to dress, something she had no trouble doing quickly. Bridget believed in a simple wardrobe—blue jeans, blue canvas sneakers, a white T-shirt, a navy blue sweatshirt, and her ubiquitous Yankees' cap. Of course, somehow, this morning, all her blue sweatshirts were in the laundry, and she had to settle for a gray one, with a zipper and a hood. Bridget put on the sweatshirt and zipped it up. It didn't look right. She unzipped it. Not great, but better.

She'd have to zip the sweatshirt up when she left the apartment to please her mother. She could unzip it again outside.

Almost ready to leave, Bridget went back into the bathroom for her final chore: Brushing her teeth. Her dentist had criticized her on her last visit for doing a slapdash job of brushing and neglecting to floss. Apparently, her laziness had resulted in her first cavity. So now she took special care in angling the brush toward her gums, brushing every tooth gently but firmly, and flossing afterwards the way the dentist had shown her.

Putting her toothbrush back, Bridget hurried to her room to grab her book bag and flew to the front door. "'Bye, Mom!" Bridget called out. She was waiting for the elevator when her mother stuck her head out the door.

"You forgot to replace the toothpaste cap again, Sweetie," her mother said.

The elevator door opened. "But, Mom, I'm gonna be late!" Bridget complained. "It's the first day."

Bridget's mother looked at the ceiling. "How do we learn to put the toothpaste cap back on the toothpaste?" she asked.

Bridget trudged back to the front door and past her mother. "We make ourselves late by having to go back."

"Why do we put the cap back on?" Bridget's mother continued.

In the bathroom, Bridget screwed the cap back on and raced back to the front door. "Because if we don't, the toothpaste dries out." She made a great show of pressing the elevator button again.

"Have a great day, Sweetie," her mother said. "Don't chew too much gum." She went inside and closed the door.

When the elevator arrived, Bridget looked at her watch. She had ten minutes to get to school, and a twenty-minute trip from door to door. Pretty simple math. She sighed and unzipped her sweatshirt.

Let's concentrate on the first two lines of the passage. In this one sentence, there are three ideas expressed, two major ideas and a minor one. The first idea is that Bridget woke up early:

Bridget got up in plenty of time to make it to school early on Monday,

The second idea is introduced by the word *but*:

but . . . something happened between the time she got up and when she left the apartment.

The second major idea in the sentence is that, while she may have woken up early, Bridget's going to be late for school anyway. What can make a sentence like this confusing is the part in the middle, the minor idea that separates the two major ones:

as was generally the case,

The point of this little fragment is that Bridget is almost *always* late for school, because something always "happens" to make her late. As the passage goes on to explain, she lingers over breakfast, she's a slow bather, and her simple way of dressing doesn't necessarily save her time.

That's how a straightedge, by helping you to concentrate on one line at a time, can break up sentences and communicate their separate, sometimes contradictory, ideas to you.

✍ DRILL #10A ✍

Answer these questions about the passage.

1. What is foremost in Bridget's mind this morning?

   a. being on time for school

   b. having lunch with Babette

   c. the Yankees' loss to the Brewers

2. Why is Bridget chronically late?

   a. her routine is inefficient

   b. her appetite is huge

   c. her mother makes her put the toothpaste cap back on

3. What is generally the dominant color in Bridget's wardrobe?

   a. gray

   b. red

   c. blue

4. Who has criticized Bridget lately?

   a. her mother

   b. her teacher

   c. her dentist

5. Who would Bridget replace Jorge Posada with if she managed the Yankees?

   a. Stan Musial

   b. Mike Stanley

   c. Joe Torre

The answers can be found on page 172.

✍PASSAGE #10B✎

Read the following passage and take notes on whatever strikes you about it. The notes can record aspects of Bridget's life and character, facts about the location of the action, or anything else.

Bridget left her parents' building and walked down Eighty-sixth Street toward the subway. It was only three blocks, but they were long blocks and seemed especially long on days when she was late. It was another pretty, New York autumn day, but of course she couldn't enjoy it very much. All she could think of was getting to class in the middle of roll call, easing the door open, shutting it gently behind her, and having to find an empty seat that wasn't in the first row without calling attention to herself. She hoped the teacher would be kind and not single her out.

Finally, Bridget reached the subway on Broadway and went down the steps. There was a long line for the token booth, and Bridget was glad that she had a student pass. She got it out of her wallet and froze. It was last year's pass and wasn't valid anymore. This was the first day of school, when the new passes would be handed out. Bridget got on the end of the line for tokens and tried to control her anger.

The line moved slowly, and when Bridget was one person away from the window, a downtown local pulled into the station. Her train. She turned back to the window and tried to will the token clerk to work faster, but the person in front of Bridget had a twenty-dollar bill and only wanted one token. The token clerk could only count out $18.50 just so quickly. When he was done, the other person left the token window and Bridget slipped her dollar and two quarters through the slot. A token slid back through and Bridget palmed it, turning and rushing to the turnstiles.

Another traffic jam. Bridget had to stop short to avoid colliding with a man having a hard time with his computerized fare card. Whether his account was overdrawn, the machine was broken, or he just didn't know how to use the card—it didn't matter. He wasn't budging until he had tried it a few more times. "This is why I prefer tokens," thought Bridget, who had been a subway rider for years before fare cards were introduced and was against them in principle. She managed to keep her feelings to herself.

The turnstile next to the first one was clogged by a woman who could not seem to maneuver her five large shopping bags through the small space. The next was blocked by a couple who were kissing each other goodbye as though they wouldn't see each other again for many years. Was the man going off to war or, Bridget hoped, jail? Was the woman? While blocking a turnstile during rush hour seemed to justify some sort of punishment, Bridget realized it wasn't her place to decide what that punishment should be. So, she let it go. "As a gesture to love," she thought.

The fourth turnstile was clear, and Bridget wheeled through it like the veteran she was. Glancing to her right, she saw the local, its doors standing open three tracks and two platforms away. Bridget took off for the down staircase and took the fifteen steps in groups of three. She hit the ground running and mounted the up staircase on the fly. Halfway up, caught behind a slow-moving older gentleman, Bridget heard the dreaded sound: Ding dong! The doors were closing. There was no squeezing around the man without slamming her book bag into him. So Bridget maintained his pace until they reached the top of the stairs, where Bridget watched unsurprised as the local slipped away out of the station.

The next train took no more than five minutes to arrive, but it seemed like half an hour. The doors opened and Bridget squeezed into the car, which was packed to the gills near the doors, and open and spacious in the middle. Bridget took off her book bag and squirmed and slithered her way to the middle of the car, where she grabbed onto a pole and shut her eyes.

What does the passage tell us about Bridget? Well, for one thing, she lives on Eighty-sixth Street. This doesn't mean much to anyone who doesn't live in New York, but it may prove significant later on. You never know. Another thing about Bridget is sort of the point of the passage: She has very definite ideas about subway etiquette. These ideas can be broken up into a list of subway don'ts: don't pay for one token with a twenty-dollar bill (if you can help it), don't use a computerized fare card unless you know how it works, don't kiss goodbye in front of the turnstile, don't stand in the doorway of a subway car.

Your notes may include other things that seemed significant to you. It doesn't matter what you include in your mind, as long as it helps keep you involved in the story, and embeds the points the author has tried to make.

✍DRILL #10B✍

Answer the following questions about the passage.

1. Why is it so hard for Bridget to walk three blocks to the subway?

    a. She has a pebble in her shoe.

    b. People keep getting in her way.

    c. The walk seems longer than it is because she's late.

2. Bridget's theory of subway etiquette is designed to

    a. get her to school faster today

    b. make subway riding more efficient for everyone

    c. put inconsiderate people in prison

3. Why does Bridget dislike computerized fare cards?

    a. because they don't work

    b. because they cost more than tokens

    c. because she started riding the subway before the era of fare cards

4. Why must Bridget slow down on the up-staircase and miss her train?

   a. because there is one person in front of her on the right and one on the left

   b. because the doors are already closing and it's no use

   c. because to hit the man in front of her with her book bag would undermine her theory of subway etiquette

5. Is Bridget being unreasonable in her rage toward rude subway riders?

   a. yes, she thinks they should go to prison

   b. no, she thinks they should use tokens

   c. no, she makes exceptions for people who are in love

The answers can be found on page 173.

✍ DRILL #10C ✎

Here are some vocabulary words taken from chapters 1–9. Try to match each word up with its synonym.

1. abide	____		a.	temperament
2. illustrious	____		b.	visit
3. disposition	____		c.	starving
4. forbidding	____		d.	irritate
5. maul	____		e.	renowned
6. desist	____		f.	unpleasant
7. hokum	____		g.	shrink
8. sojourn	____		h.	hateful
9. crestfallen	____		i.	meditation
10. exploit	____		j.	stop
11. ravenous	____		k.	tremble
12. chafe	____		l.	remain
13. unsavory	____		m.	calmness
14. nonchalant	____		n.	scoundrel
15. blackguard	____		o.	injure
16. composure	____		p.	indifferent
17. quaver	____		q.	nonsense
18. rumination	____		r.	dejected
19. odious	____		s.	threatening
20. dwindle	____		t.	feat

The answers can be found on page 173.

✍ DRILL #10D ✍

Complete the following sentences.

1. "It would _____ you to wear a motorcycle helmet if you're going skiing," Mom said.

   a. behoove

   b. indulge

   c. revel

2. The moon is waning tonight; in a _____ it will be full.

   a. torrent

   b. magnate

   c. fortnight

3. The strange whistle Joe Bob found was only _____ to his dog, who writhed in pain on the ground whenever it was blown.

   a. ample

   b. boorish

   c. audible

4. Frank travels everywhere with an _____ : He has one guy to carry his money, another to dial the phone, and another to cut up his steak.

   a. adversary

   b. entourage

   c. emphasis

5. Your tuxedo gives me the _____ impression that you are going to the ballet.

   a. dutiful

   b. distinct

   c. dilapidated

6. When I kicked in Buddy's TV screen, he seemed
_____ rather than angry.

   a. bewildered

   b. bedraggled

   c. leery

7. After his _____ in the army, Doug settled down
to a pleasant life of gardening and speaking in funny
voices.

   a. thoroughfare

   b. tarpaulin

   c. stint

8. "Your fly is open," she said, but I could barely hear
her above the _____ of my boombox.

   a. din

   b. jargon

   c. buffoon

9. I must confess I _____ doubts about your plan
to become a professional eunuch.

   a. languish

   b. harbor

   c. revile

10. _____ of energy, I couldn't even move from the
floor to the couch.

   a. Solicitous

   b. Blustery

   c. Bereft

11. Perhaps, instead of buying this solid gold coffee table, I should put the money in a savings account and let it _____ interest.

    a. commence

    b. constitute

    c. accumulate

12. The customs inspector said that, if we didn't stop repeating everything he said in high-pitched voices, he would _____ our passports.

    a. teem

    b. rescind

    c. cajole

13. The _____ laughter from the fraternity brothers at the next table made us grind our teeth.

    a. raucous

    b. scandalous

    c. surreptitious

14. The rock star was beautifully _____ in a puffy, royal blue down jacket and matching sweatpants.

    a. meticulous

    b. prim

    c. attired

15. I would prefer to be _____ , but my boss wants me in the office from nine to five.

    a. flabbergasted

    b. shod

    c. nocturnal

16. The police ordered us to _____ the premises, or they would send in the clowns.

    a. vacate

    b. wrest

    c. admonish

17. I don't mean to _____ , but my bear did beat your gorilla pretty handily.

    a. hail

    b. gloat

    c. invoke

18. Come over for some pancakes, if you're so _____.

    a. disillusioned

    b. inclined

    c. induced

19. If you want to be a _____ , you must be prepared to spend a lot of time in court.

    a. varmint

    b. curator

    c. felon

20. The principal _____ on me, because I once got his burrito away from a Doberman.

    a. abides

    b. dotes

    c. importunes

The answers can be found on page 173.

Chapter 11
Answer Key

Drill #1 (from page 8)

1. Compucon; chairman and chief executive officer
2. The ballroom of the Compucon Marquis Hotel
3. Shorten
4. Convert every book ever written so that it can only be read on a computer screen, so he can sell more computers and make more money
5. There is no opinion given. Straight news reporters are not supposed to give their opinions in their articles.

Drill #2 (from page 18)

1. No time; it is instantaneous
2. A large trunk of lightning forking out into many branches
3. Light
4. The angry roars of the gods
5. Count the number of seconds between the sight of the lightning flash and the sound of the thunder. Divide that number by five, and the resulting number is the distance away, in miles, of the storm.

Drill #3 (from page 30)

1. The basement of the New York Public Library
2. It's classical music.
3. A rhinoceros and a pig (swine)
4. He thinks Dean O'Malley told the kids about the Continuum
5. White

Drill #4 (from page 43)
1. 50
2. Rags, broken shoes, and a slouch hat
3. A tree toad and a fish belly
4. Beat
5. A bad one; they're like remote acquaintances who don't like each other

Drill #5 (from page 62)
1. a
2. Amy
3. c
4. c
5. b

Drill #6 (from page 80)
1. b
2. c
3. a
4. c
5. b

Drill #7 (from page 101)
1. c
2. a
3. b
4. b
5. c

Drill #8 (from page 123)
1. b
2. c
3. a
4. c
5. a

Drill #9 (from page 151)
1. c
2. a
3. b
4. c
5. b

Drill #10a (from page 159)
1. c
2. a
3. c
4. c
5. b

Drill #10b (from page 162)
1. c
2. b
3. c
4. c
5. c

Drill #10c (from page 163)

1. l
2. e
3. a
4. s
5. o
6. j
7. q
8. b
9. r
10. t
11. c
12. d
13. f
14. p
15. n
16. m
17. k
18. i
19. h
20. g

Drill #10d (from page 164)

1. a
2. c
3. c
4. b
5. b
6. a
7. c
8. a
9. b
10. c
11. c
12. b
13. a
14. c
15. c
16. a
17. b
18. b
19. c
20. b

ABOUT THE AUTHOR

Bruno Blumenfeld attended the State University of New York at Binghamton and the School of Visual Arts. He lives in New York City.

FIND US...

International

Hong Kong
4/F Sun Hung Kai Centre
30 Harbour Road, Wan Chai,
Hong Kong
Tel: (011)85-2-517-3016

Japan
Fuji Building 40, 15-14
Sakuragaokacho, Shibuya Ku,
Tokyo 150, Japan
Tel: (011)81-3-3463-1343

Korea
Tae Young Bldg, 944-24,
Daechi- Dong, Kangnam-Ku
The Princeton Review- ANC
Seoul, Korea 135-280,
South Korea
Tel: (011)82-2-554-7763

Mexico City
PR Mex S De RL De Cv
Guanajuato 228 Col. Roma
06700 Mexico D.F., Mexico
Tel: 525-564-9468

Montreal
666 Sherbrooke St.
West, Suite 202
Montreal, QC H3A 1E7 Canada
Tel: (514) 499-0870

Pakistan
1 Bawa Park - 90 Upper Mall
Lahore, Pakistan
Tel: (011)92-42-571-2315

Spain
Pza. Castilla, 3 - 5° A, 28046
Madrid, Spain
Tel: (011)341-323-4212

Taiwan
155 Chung Hsiao East Road
Section 4 - 4th Floor,
Taipei R.O.C., Taiwan
Tel: (011)886-2-751-1243

Thailand
Building One, 99 Wireless Road
Bangkok, Thailand 10330
Tel: (662) 256-7080

Toronto
1240 Bay Street, Suite 300
Toronto M5R 2A7 Canada
Tel: (800) 495-7737
Tel: (716) 839-4391

Vancouver
4212 University Way NE,
Suite 204
Seattle, WA 98105
Tel: (206) 548-1100

National (U.S.)
We have over 60 offices around the U.S. and
run courses in over 400 sites. For courses and locations
within the U.S. call 1 (800) 2/Review and you will be
routed to the nearest office.

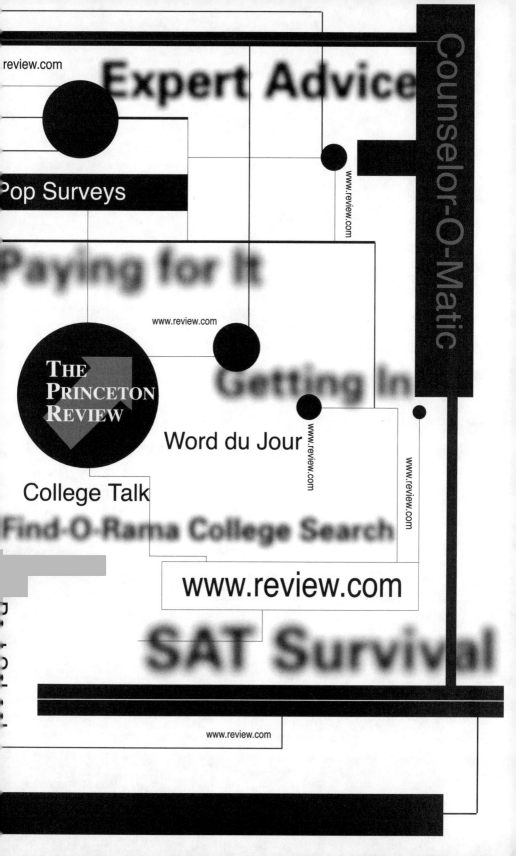